Embracing Emotions

In Search of Inner Balance

Content

Happiness — 1-6 pag
The Magical Journey of the Gleeful Smiles

Sadness — 7-14 pag
The Journey of Emotion's Light in the Forest of Smiles

Anger — 15-22 pag
The Mystery of Color Clash

Fear — 23-31 pag
Journey of Spark and the Light of Friendship

Disgust — 32-42 pag
Luca's Story & The Jungle

Emotion of Surprise — 43-48 pag
A Day Full of Surprises in the Land of Smiles

The emotion of contempt — 49-56 pag
The Story of the Disgusting Flower

Happiness

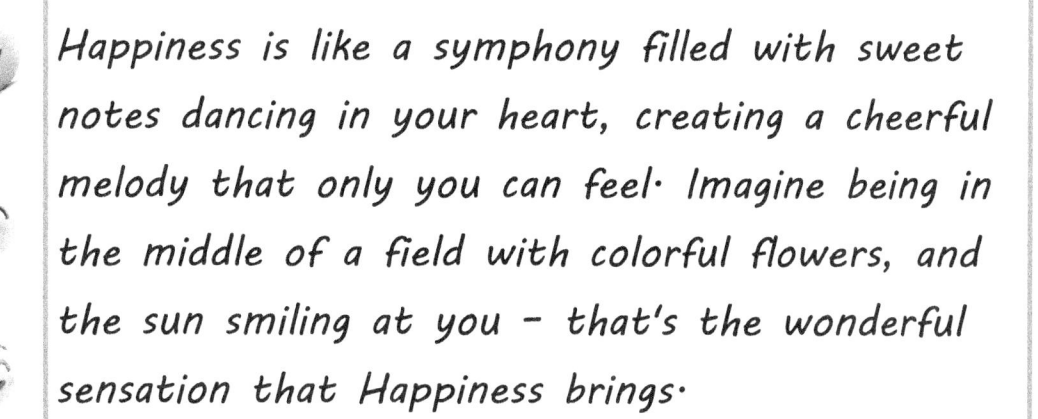

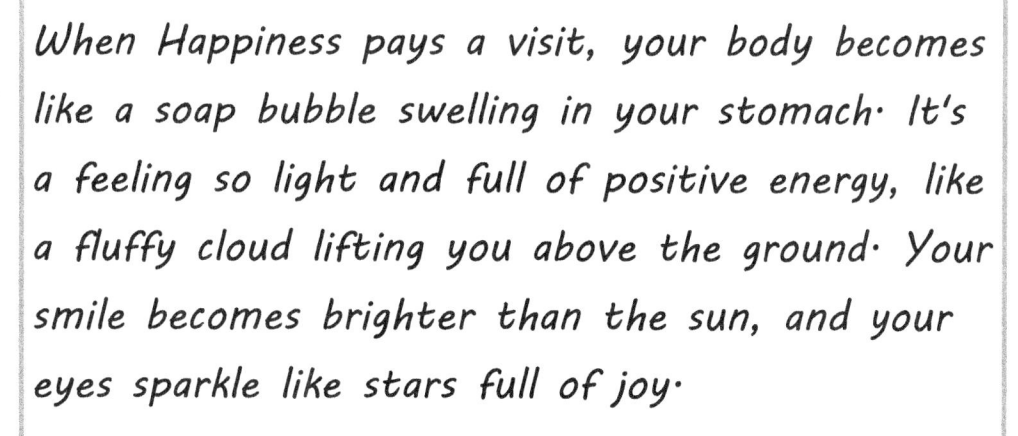

Happiness is like a symphony filled with sweet notes dancing in your heart, creating a cheerful melody that only you can feel. Imagine being in the middle of a field with colorful flowers, and the sun smiling at you - that's the wonderful sensation that Happiness brings.

When Happiness pays a visit, your body becomes like a soap bubble swelling in your stomach. It's a feeling so light and full of positive energy, like a fluffy cloud lifting you above the ground. Your smile becomes brighter than the sun, and your eyes sparkle like stars full of joy.

Every part of you becomes a little dancer in this symphony of happiness. You may feel your feet wanting to jump for joy or your hands wanting to embrace the whole world. You can't stay still because you're overwhelmed by the need to share this joy with everyone around.

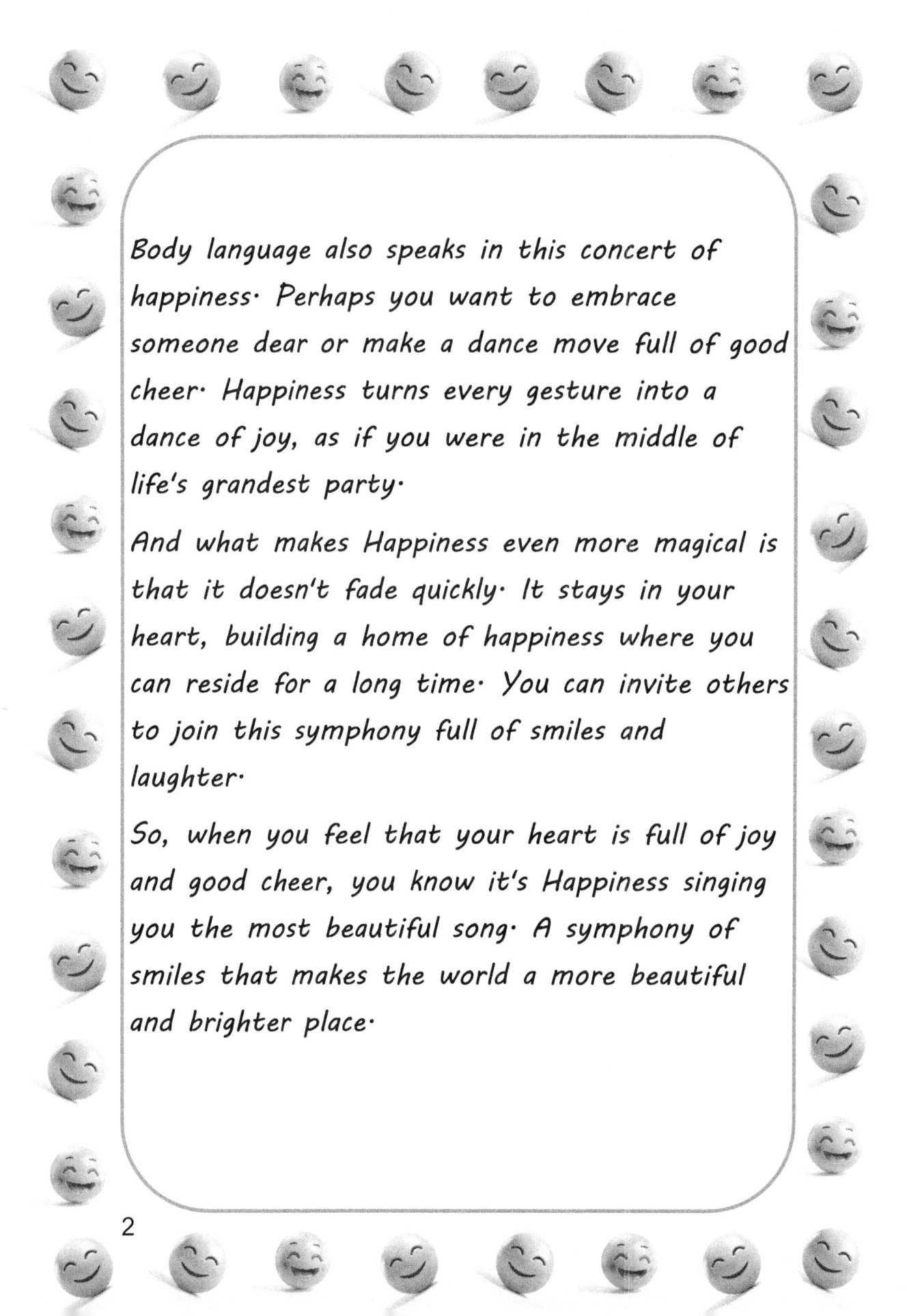

Body language also speaks in this concert of happiness. Perhaps you want to embrace someone dear or make a dance move full of good cheer. Happiness turns every gesture into a dance of joy, as if you were in the middle of life's grandest party.

And what makes Happiness even more magical is that it doesn't fade quickly. It stays in your heart, building a home of happiness where you can reside for a long time. You can invite others to join this symphony full of smiles and laughter.

So, when you feel that your heart is full of joy and good cheer, you know it's Happiness singing you the most beautiful song. A symphony of smiles that makes the world a more beautiful and brighter place.

Tips for Managing the Emotion of Happiness and Joy

Smile and Laugh

When you feel happy, smile and laugh heartily! A smile can make the world seem more beautiful.

Share Your Joy

Tell your friends or family about the things that make you happy. By sharing your joy, you can make others smile too.
Keep Dear Memories:

Draw or write about the happy moments you have. You can create an album with pictures or drawings that remind you of those beautiful moments.

Play and Have Fun

Join in games and activities that make you feel good. Happiness can be found in a fun game or in playtime with friends.
Be Thankful for Small Things:

Be grateful for the small things around you that bring happiness. A flutter of butterflies or a delicious chocolate can be reasons for joy.

Be Kind to Others

Help your friends or share your toys with those around you. Kind gestures bring joy and make your heart feel full of happiness.

Create Beautiful Things

Draw, paint, or create something beautiful. Creative projects can bring great satisfaction and make you very happy.

Spending Time in Nature

Take a walk in the park or go on a nature hike. Fresh air and the beauty of nature can bring a sense of happiness.

Listen to Upbeat Music

Listen to tunes that make you feel good and dance. Upbeat rhythms can lift any mood.

Be Grateful for Friends

Friends are a treasure! Be thankful for your friends and spend time with them, as they often bring the greatest happiness.

Learn to Enjoy Simple Things and Share Your Happiness with Those Around You. Each Day Brings Opportunities to Feel Joy and Make the Surrounding World Happier!

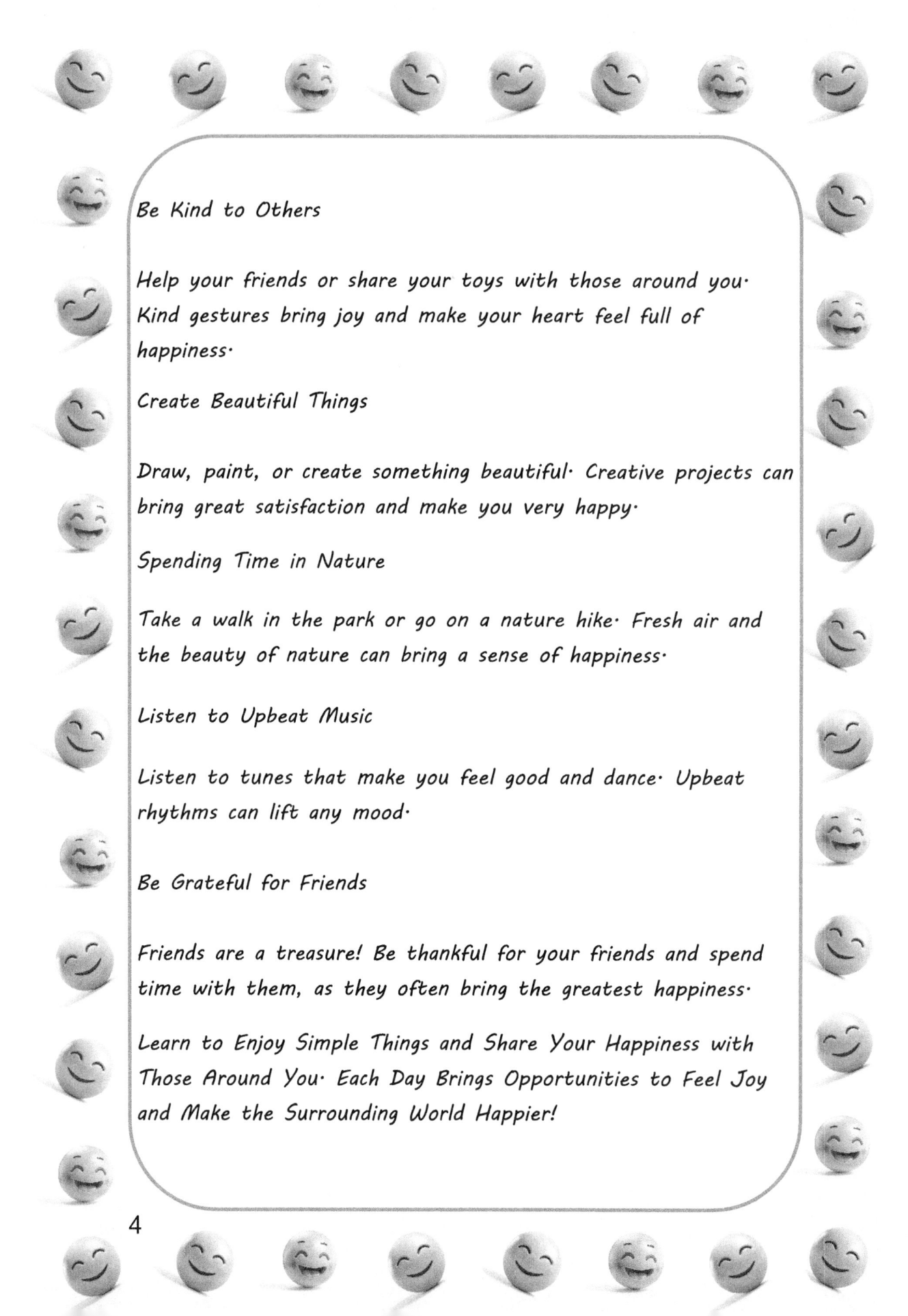

The Magical Journey of the Gleeful Smiles

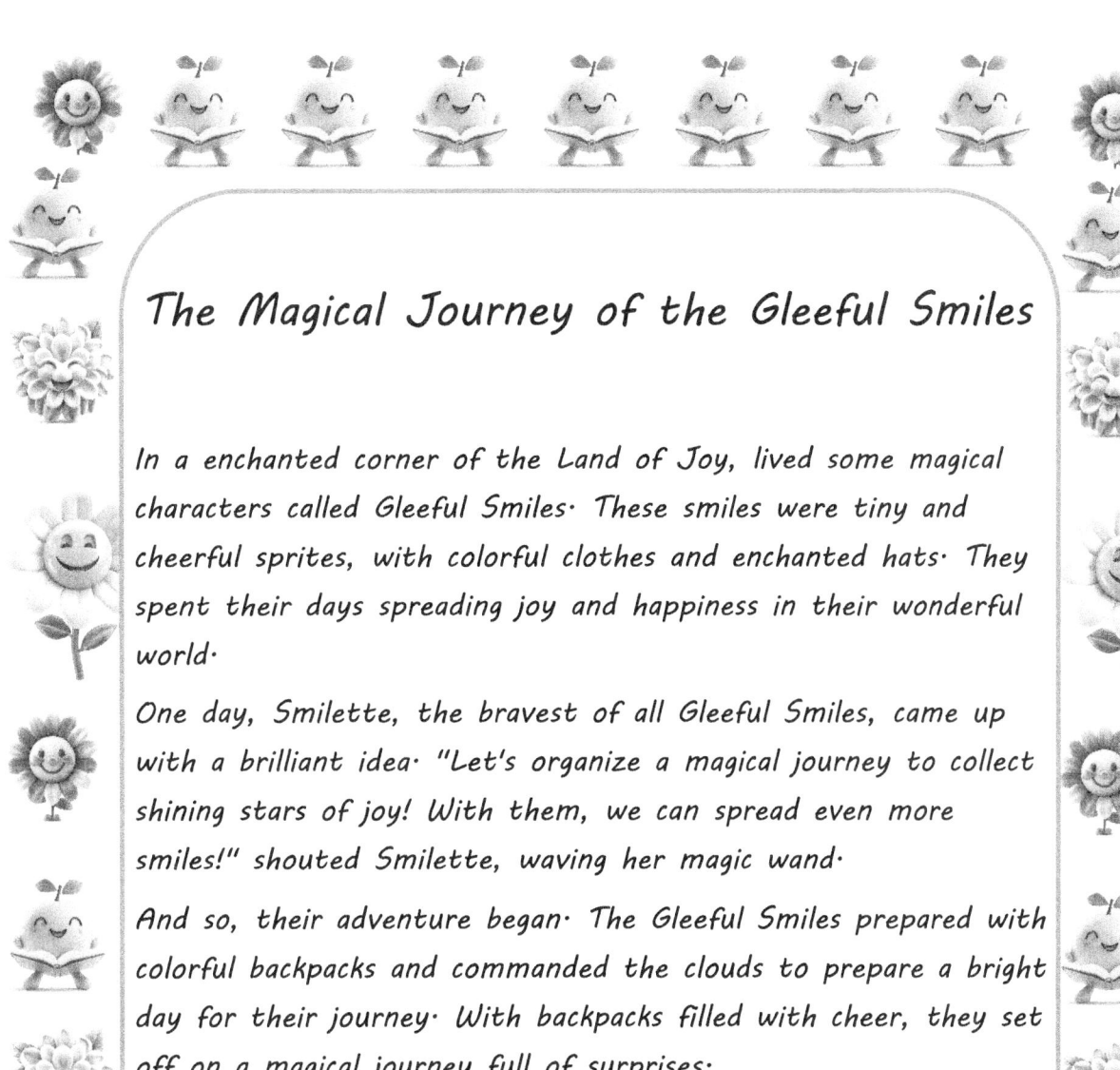

In a enchanted corner of the Land of Joy, lived some magical characters called Gleeful Smiles. These smiles were tiny and cheerful sprites, with colorful clothes and enchanted hats. They spent their days spreading joy and happiness in their wonderful world.

One day, Smilette, the bravest of all Gleeful Smiles, came up with a brilliant idea. "Let's organize a magical journey to collect shining stars of joy! With them, we can spread even more smiles!" shouted Smilette, waving her magic wand.

And so, their adventure began. The Gleeful Smiles prepared with colorful backpacks and commanded the clouds to prepare a bright day for their journey. With backpacks filled with cheer, they set off on a magical journey full of surprises.

Their first stop was the Garden of Joy, where flowers danced to the rhythm of their laughter. The Gleeful Smiles started singing joyful songs, and the flowers began to bloom and dance in a show of colors and delightful scents.

Then they headed to the Lake of Laughter, a enchanted place where children's laughter gathered and turned into sparkling rivers. The Gleeful Smiles jumped on cloud bridges and began to collect drops of laughter to share with those who needed a splash of happiness.

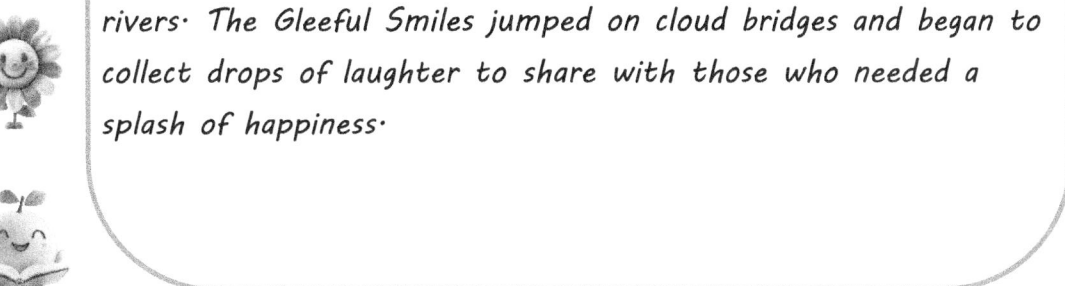

On their way, they passed through the Forest of Giggles, where trees whispered funny stories, and birds sang melodies full of good cheer. The Gleeful Smiles collected giggles from the air and shared them with children who wanted to laugh even more.

When they reached the Summit of Smiles, they discovered a magical place from where they could see the entire Land of Joy. The Gleeful Smiles tossed their backpacks into the air, and the sparkling stars of joy fell like a golden rain, covering everything around with the brilliance of happiness.

After a day full of adventures, the Gleeful Smiles returned to their home with hearts full of joy and backpacks filled with magical stars. They shared these stars with all the residents of the Land of Joy, and every person who received a star felt a special warmth in their heart and a magical smile on their lips.

And so, the Gleeful Smiles learned that happiness is like a magical journey, and joy gathers from every corner of the world. With every laugh and every shared smile, the world became a brighter and happier place.

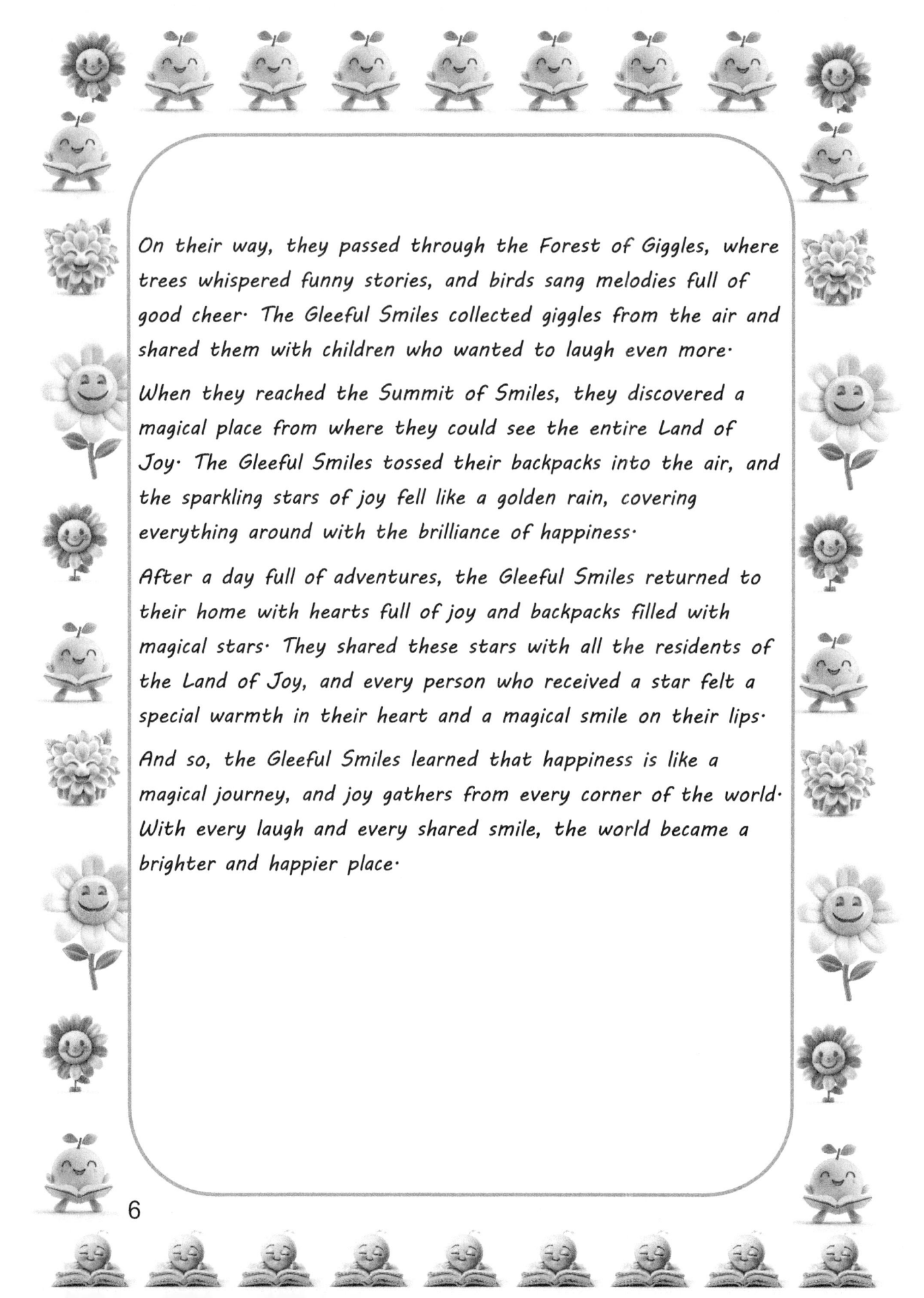

Sadness

Sadness is like an autumn rain dripping slowly on the window, bringing with it a sense of melancholy and heaviness in the heart. It's an emotion many of us experience at some point in life, and it's important to understand it and know how to manage it.

When we're sad, we feel a lump in our throat and a weight in our chest, as if our heart is heavier than usual. Sometimes, we feel tired and lacking in energy, and activities that normally bring us joy seem to hold no appeal.

On our face, sadness is evident through teary eyes and lost looks, as if we're searching for something we can't find. Our lips may be downturned, and our usual smile may be absent, replaced by an expression of sorrow.

Our body language also speaks of sadness. We might frown or hunch our shoulders, as if we're trying to shield ourselves from an invisible pain. Sometimes, we withdraw into ourselves and avoid eye contact with those around us.

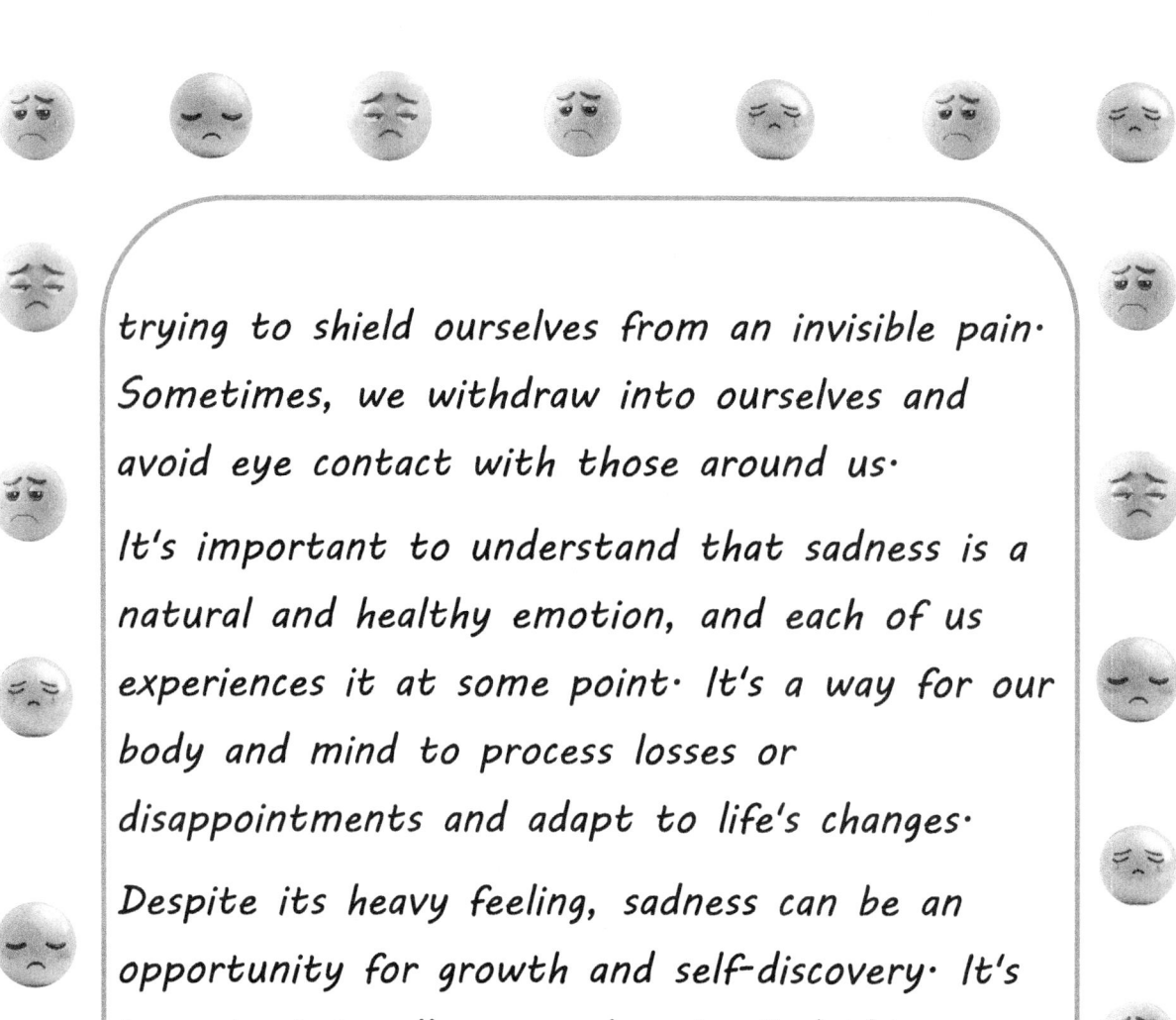

It's important to understand that sadness is a natural and healthy emotion, and each of us experiences it at some point. It's a way for our body and mind to process losses or disappointments and adapt to life's changes.

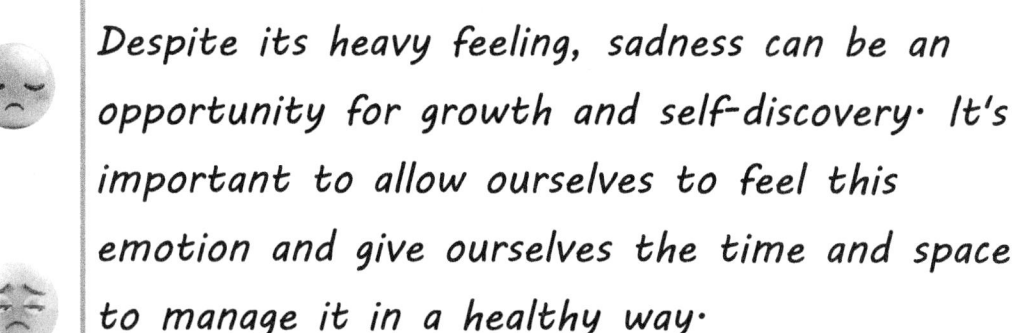

Despite its heavy feeling, sadness can be an opportunity for growth and self-discovery. It's important to allow ourselves to feel this emotion and give ourselves the time and space to manage it in a healthy way.

By accepting our sadness and seeking support from those around us, we can learn to heal and return to the light and joy of life. Remember that we're always surrounded by love and that we're not alone in our journey.

Here are Some Tips to Help You Manage Feelings of Sadness

Recognize your feelings: It's important to realize that it's perfectly normal to feel sad from time to time. You don't have to be ashamed or try to hide your sadness. Acknowledge your feelings and accept them as they are.

Talk to someone: It's helpful to share your sadness with someone you trust. It could be a friend, a family member, or a trusted adult. By talking about what makes you feel sad, you'll discover that you're not alone and that there are people who understand you and can help you.

Do something you enjoy: Try to engage in activities that bring you joy and make you feel good. It could be drawing, listening to music, playing a sport, or anything else you enjoy doing. When you immerse yourself in such activities, you'll notice that the sadness gradually fades away.

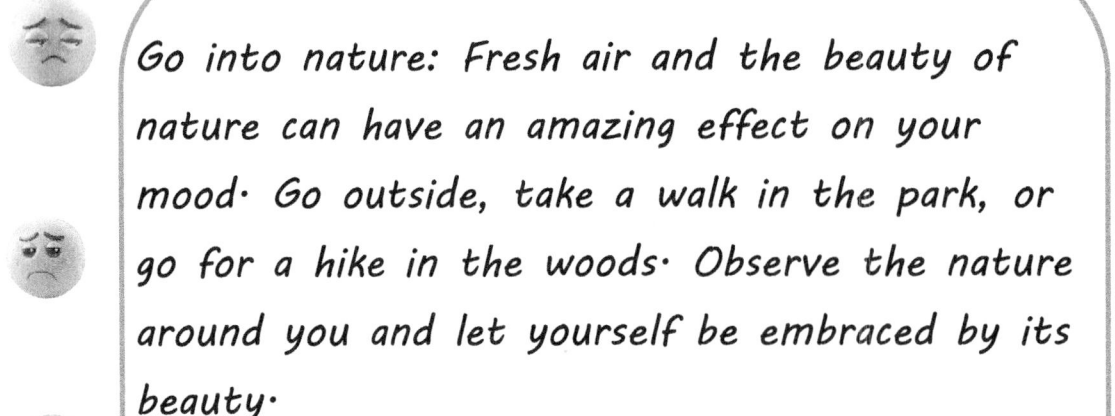

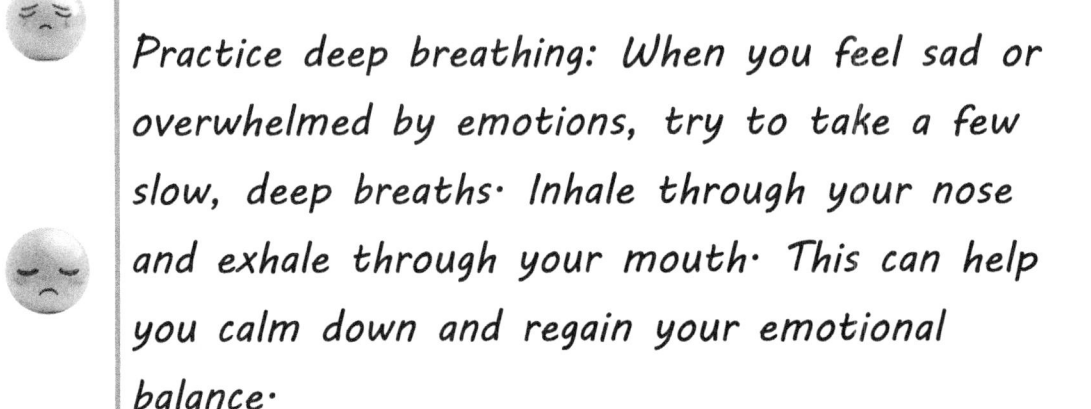

Go into nature: Fresh air and the beauty of nature can have an amazing effect on your mood. Go outside, take a walk in the park, or go for a hike in the woods. Observe the nature around you and let yourself be embraced by its beauty.

Practice deep breathing: When you feel sad or overwhelmed by emotions, try to take a few slow, deep breaths. Inhale through your nose and exhale through your mouth. This can help you calm down and regain your emotional balance.

Think positively: Encourage yourself to think positively and focus on the good things in your life. Even when things seem difficult, try to find at least one positive aspect in the situation.

Seek support: If you feel that the sadness persists and affects you seriously, don't hesitate to ask for help. You can talk to a trusted adult or seek the help of a counselor or psychologist. They are here to help you get through difficult times and regain your well-being.

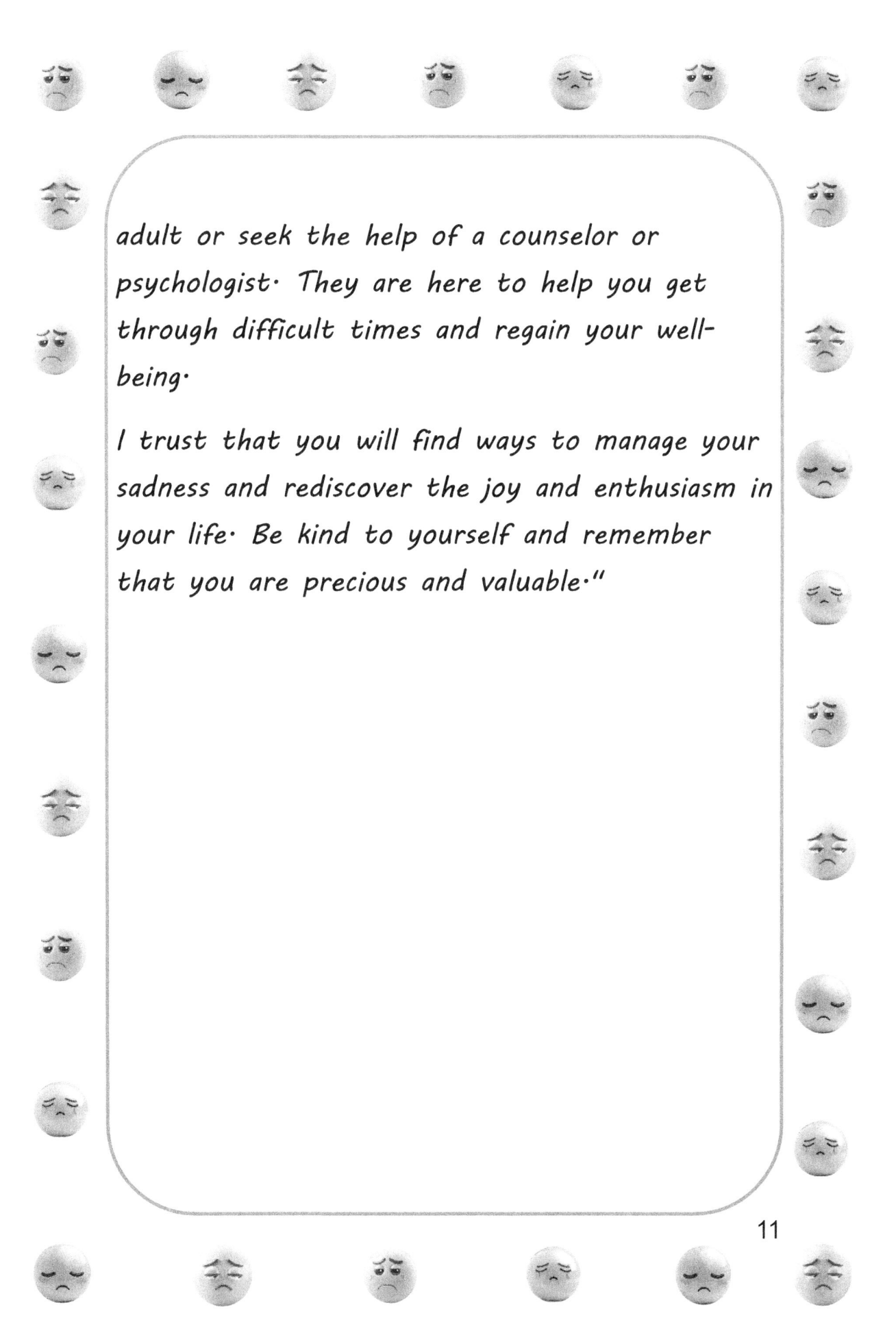

I trust that you will find ways to manage your sadness and rediscover the joy and enthusiasm in your life. Be kind to yourself and remember that you are precious and valuable."

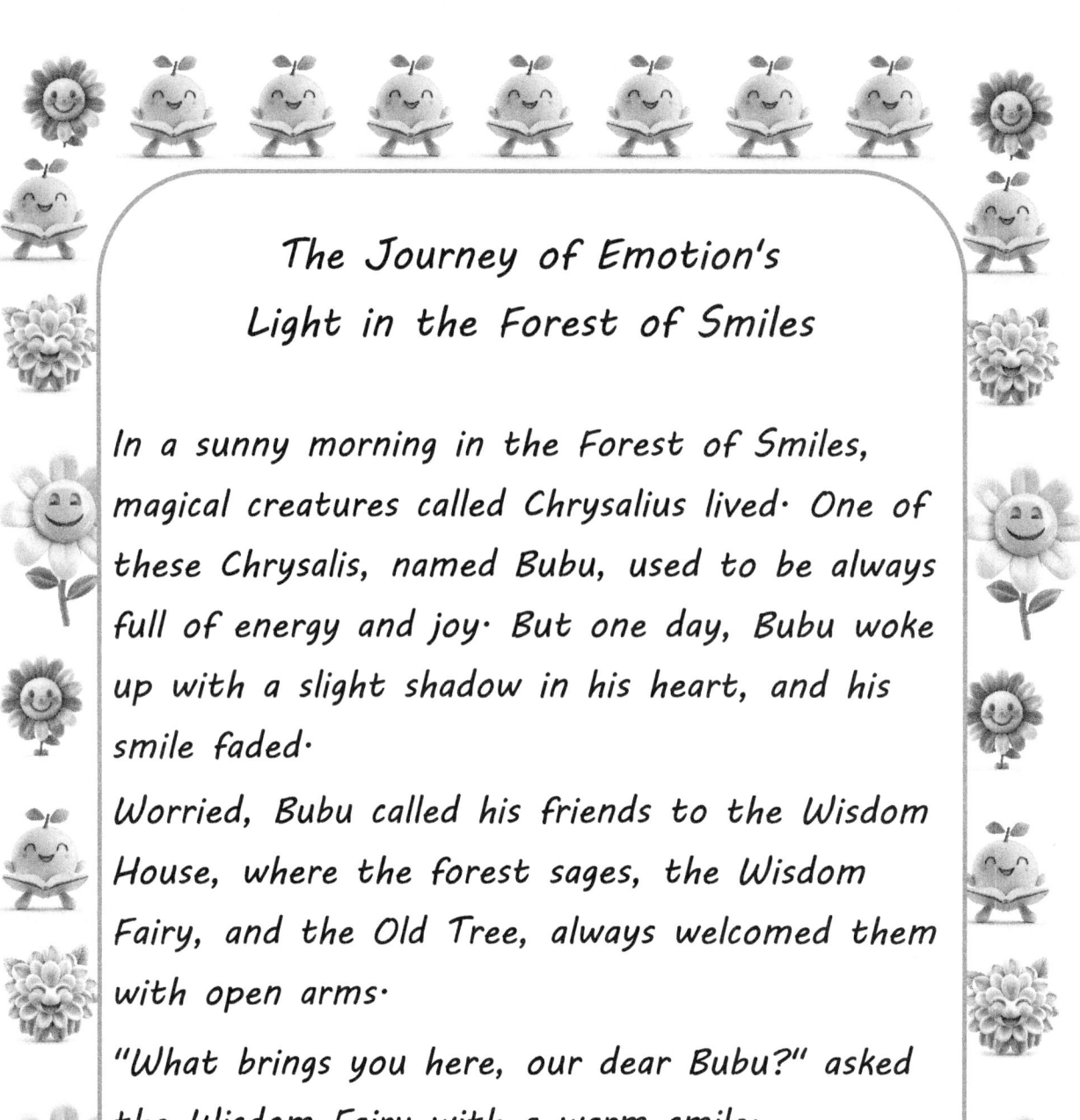

The Journey of Emotion's Light in the Forest of Smiles

In a sunny morning in the Forest of Smiles, magical creatures called Chrysalius lived. One of these Chrysalis, named Bubu, used to be always full of energy and joy. But one day, Bubu woke up with a slight shadow in his heart, and his smile faded.

Worried, Bubu called his friends to the Wisdom House, where the forest sages, the Wisdom Fairy, and the Old Tree, always welcomed them with open arms.

"What brings you here, our dear Bubu?" asked the Wisdom Fairy with a warm smile.

Bubu, looking down, confessed, "I feel sadness in my heart, and I don't understand why."

The Old Tree, with its wise leaves, invited Bubu to sit under its crown and began to talk about sadness as a natural part of life.

"Sadness, my dear Bubu, is like a drop of dew that nourishes the roots of a tree. It's important to open our hearts to understand what this emotion is telling us."

Together, they started to explore Bubu's feelings and talk about a small disappointment he had. Understanding that each sadness carries a lesson, Bubu felt his heart lightening.

The Wisdom Fairy brought a enchanted jar with threads of light and handed it to Bubu. "This is the magic jar, Bubu. When you feel overwhelmed by sadness, let it flow into these threads of light. You'll see how it transforms into wisdom and inner strength."

In the following days, Bubu used the magic jar to express his sadness. Each thread of light took on color and brilliance, and Bubu felt the emotional fatigue transforming into a deeper understanding.

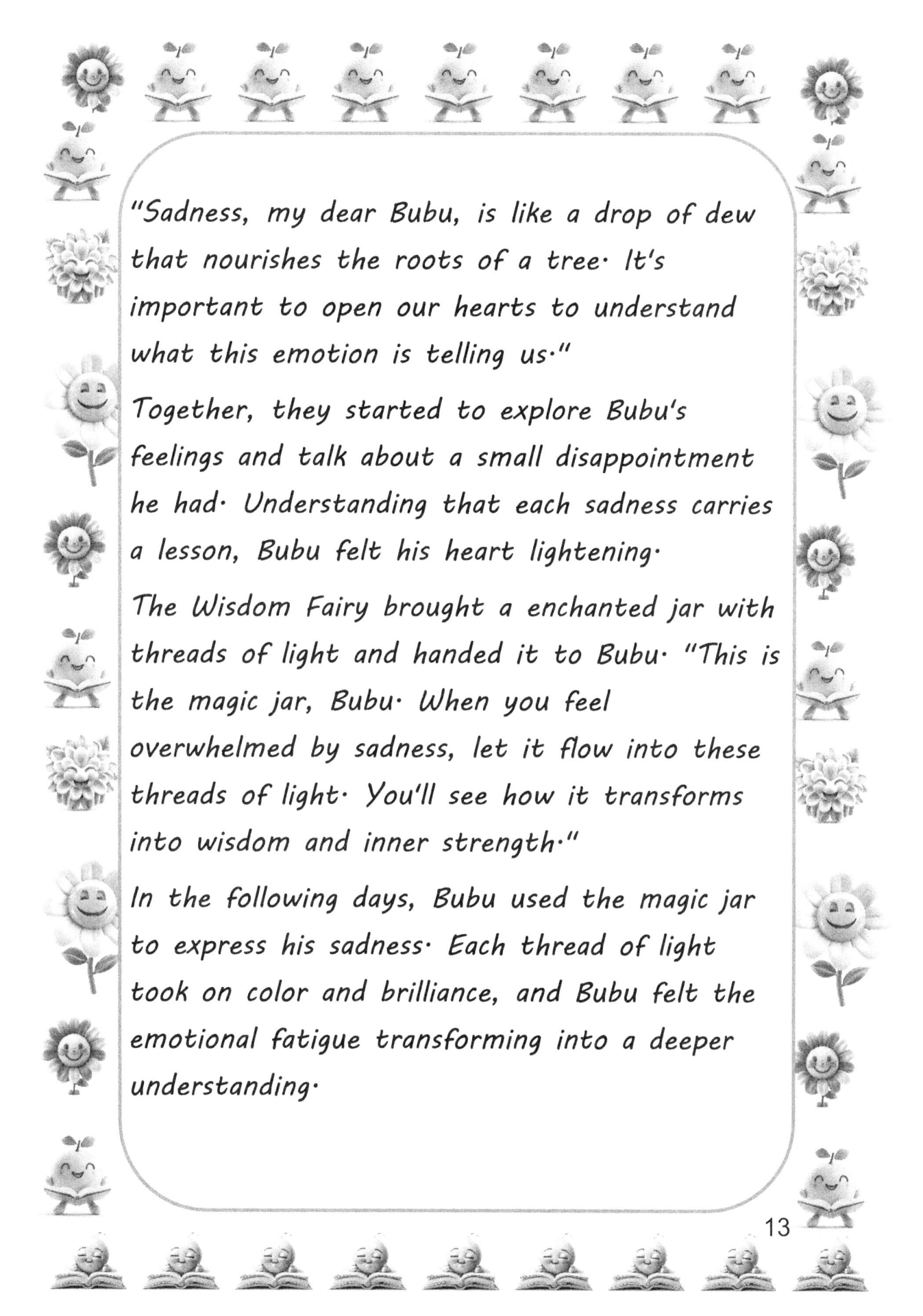

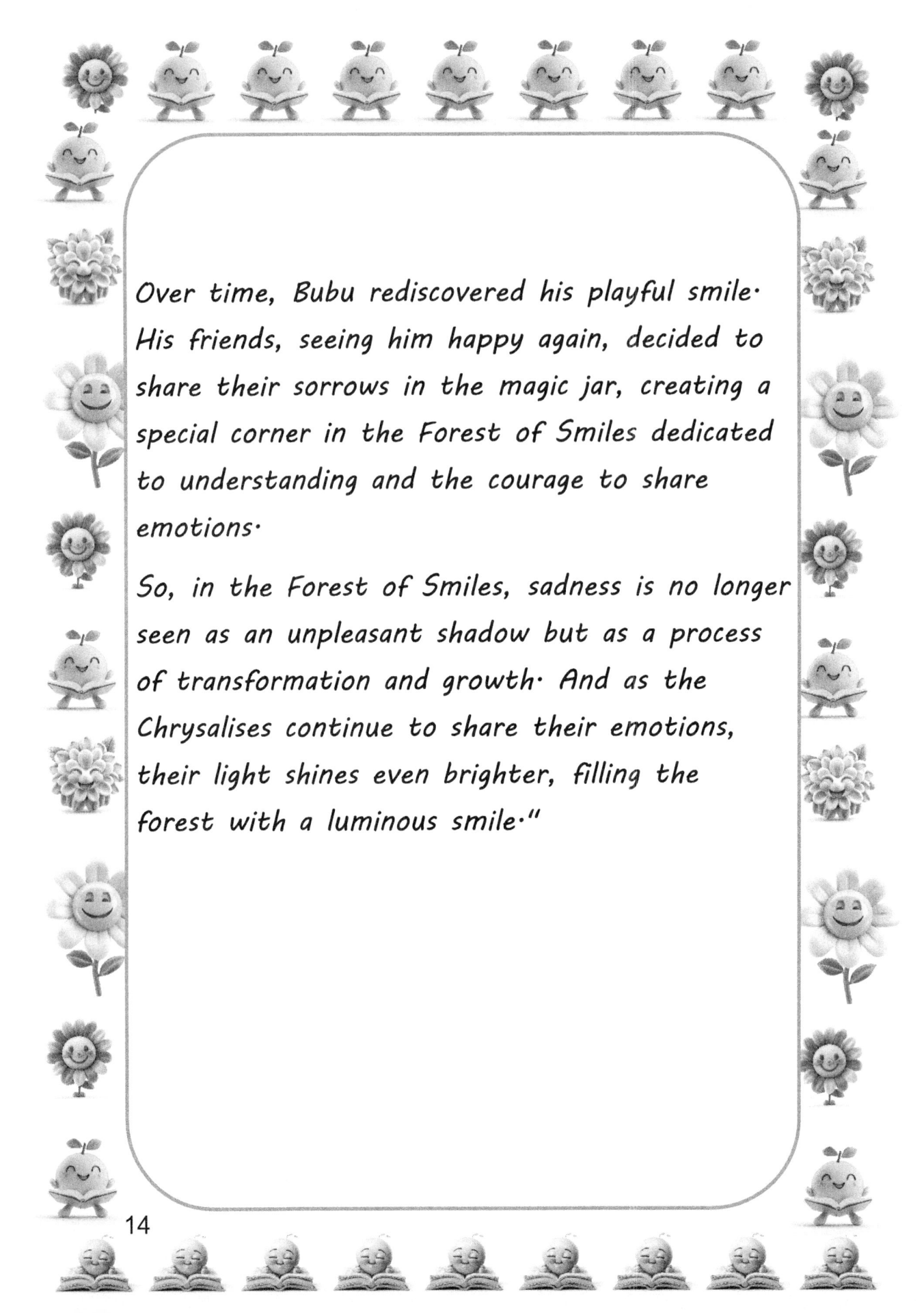

Over time, Bubu rediscovered his playful smile. His friends, seeing him happy again, decided to share their sorrows in the magic jar, creating a special corner in the Forest of Smiles dedicated to understanding and the courage to share emotions.

So, in the Forest of Smiles, sadness is no longer seen as an unpleasant shadow but as a process of transformation and growth. And as the Chrysalises continue to share their emotions, their light shines even brighter, filling the forest with a luminous smile."

Anger

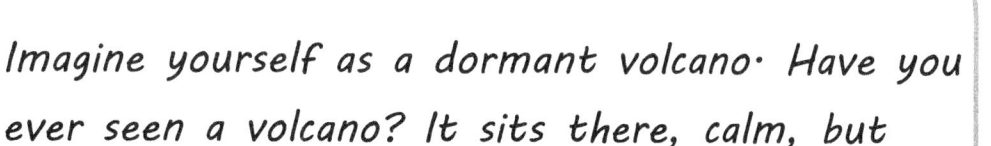

Imagine yourself as a dormant volcano. Have you ever seen a volcano? It sits there, calm, but beneath the earth's surface, it boils and prepares to erupt.

Anger is like this volcano. It's a very powerful emotion that people sometimes feel when they feel upset, wronged, or frustrated. Maybe someone took your favorite toy, maybe someone insulted you, or maybe you were treated unfairly. These are just a few examples that can awaken anger in your heart.

How do you feel anger? You feel hot inside, as if you have a small fire in your stomach that grows bigger and bigger. You feel your heart beating faster and pulsing in your ears. You can also feel yourself breathing faster, as if you were running a short distance.

How does anger show on your face? Your gaze becomes harsher, your eyebrows furrow, and your mouth becomes tight, or maybe you bite your lip nervously. Perhaps you raise your voice and say things you wouldn't normally say.

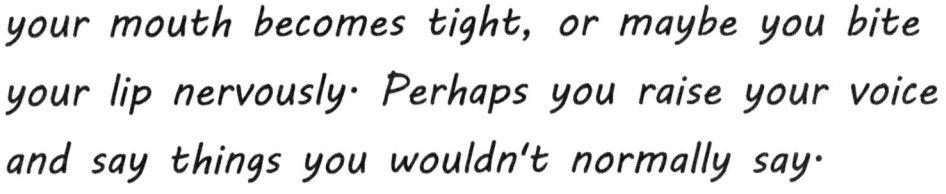

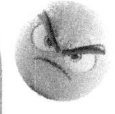

How do you recognize it in others? Here are a few signs you can observe: furrowed brows, eyes that throw sparks, or a tight mouth. Sometimes, people who are angry may seem tense and may have a raised voice.

How does it manifest in body language? Sometimes, when we're angry, we can fidget or even push or hit objects around us. We may appear stiff, and we may even seem to tense our muscles.

But what can we do when we feel anger? It's important to control our anger so that we don't harm others or ourselves. We can try to calm down by breathing deeply and counting to ten. We can talk to someone about what upset us, try to understand why we're upset, and find solutions to resolve the situation.

In conclusion, anger is like a volcano that can erupt within us, but we have the power to manage it and calm down. It's important to listen to ourselves, understand what we're feeling, and find ways to express our emotions in a healthy and constructive way.

Sometimes you may feel anger, and it's perfectly normal to feel that way. It's important to learn how to manage this anger to feel better and have better relationships with those around you. Here are some tips to help you manage your anger:

Deep and Calm Breathing: When you feel overwhelmed by anger, try to stop and take deep breaths. Inhaling and exhaling slowly can help you calm down and relax.

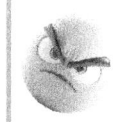

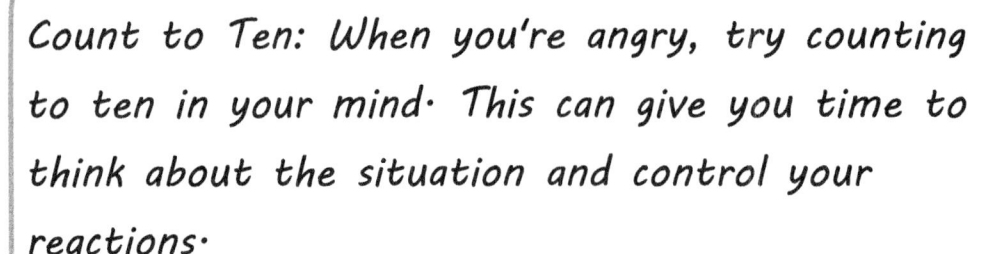

Count to Ten: When you're angry, try counting to ten in your mind. This can give you time to think about the situation and control your reactions.

Think of Solutions: Instead of focusing on what makes you angry, think about ways to solve the problem. There may be a better way to do things or to express your feelings.

Use Your Imagination: Your imagination can be a powerful tool to calm your anger. Think of a place or activity that makes you happy and imagine yourself there or doing it. It could be a walk in the park or your favorite game.

Use Art: Drawing or painting can be wonderful ways to release negative feelings. Take some paper and colored pencils and start drawing what you feel. It can be free and abstract or a representation of what makes you angry.

Music and Dance: Listen to happy music or dance in your room to release negative energy. Movement and rhythm can help you relax and feel better.

Seek Help: Remember that you have people around you who love you and can help you feel better. You can talk to your parents, teachers, or another trusted adult about how you feel and how you can manage your anger.

Play with a Pet: Pets can be very comforting and can help reduce stress and anger. Spend time with your pet and enjoy their company.

Try these tips and solutions when you feel angry, and remember that it's normal to feel these emotions. With practice and patience, you'll learn to manage your anger better and feel more calm and happy.

The Mystery of Color Clash

In a day in the Crystal Forest, Rosie and Verde, the two Curious Colts, embarked on an exciting journey to discover the hidden treasures of their enchanted realm. With fluttering tails and curious eyes, these eager friends were determined to explore every corner of the Crystal Forest.

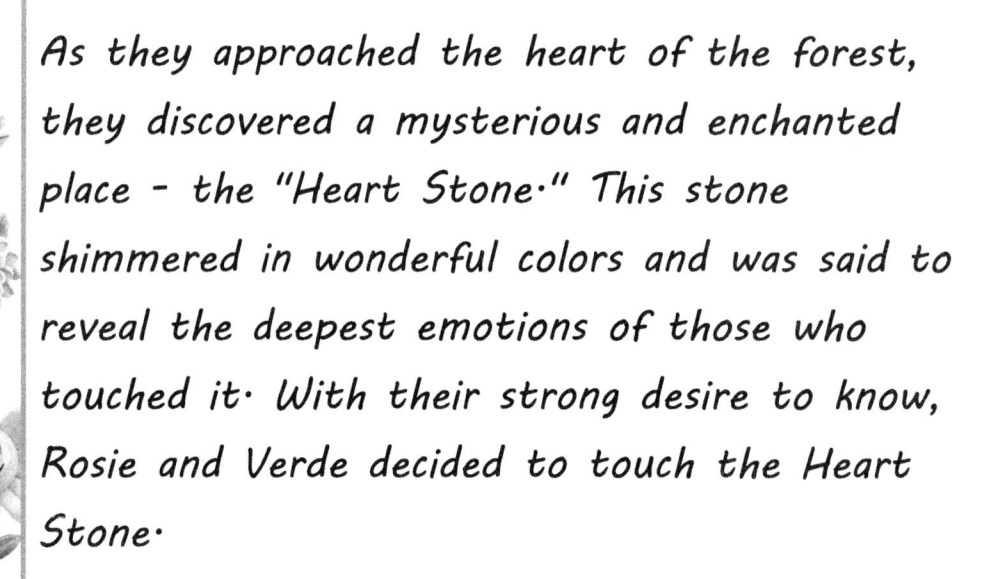

As they approached the heart of the forest, they discovered a mysterious and enchanted place - the "Heart Stone." This stone shimmered in wonderful colors and was said to reveal the deepest emotions of those who touched it. With their strong desire to know, Rosie and Verde decided to touch the Heart Stone.

At first, its colors reflected joy and curiosity, but as the Curious Colts touched the stone, they uncovered an old memory that brought them to the brink of fury. In a distant past, Rosie and Verde, then close friends, found a magic egg in the Crystal Forest. Both wanted to discover the secret of this enchanted egg, but they couldn't reach a common understanding.

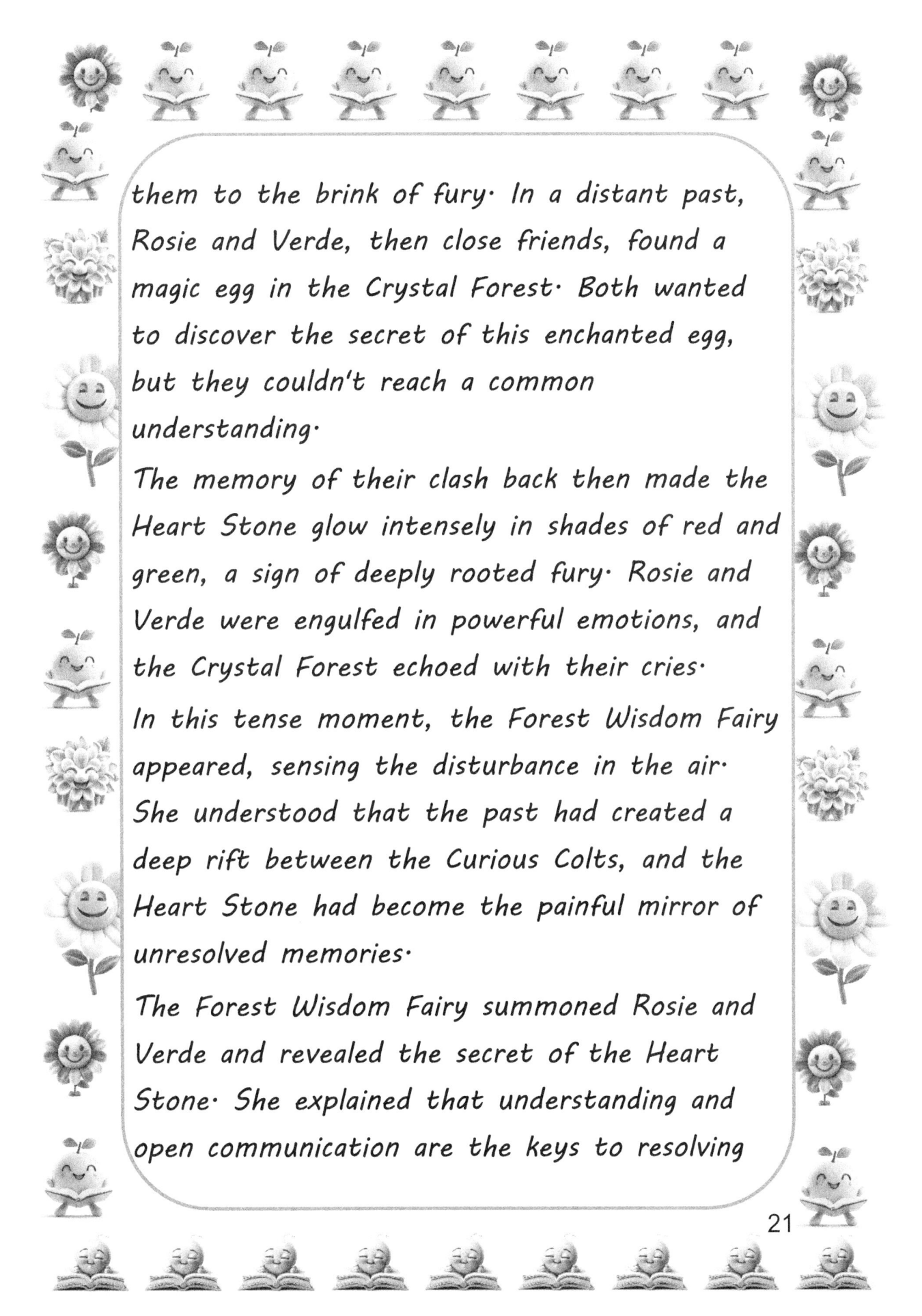

The memory of their clash back then made the Heart Stone glow intensely in shades of red and green, a sign of deeply rooted fury. Rosie and Verde were engulfed in powerful emotions, and the Crystal Forest echoed with their cries.

In this tense moment, the Forest Wisdom Fairy appeared, sensing the disturbance in the air. She understood that the past had created a deep rift between the Curious Colts, and the Heart Stone had become the painful mirror of unresolved memories.

The Forest Wisdom Fairy summoned Rosie and Verde and revealed the secret of the Heart Stone. She explained that understanding and open communication are the keys to resolving conflicts. The Fairy created a magical portal that transported them back in time to the moment of their clash over the enchanted egg. Through the portal, Rosie and Verde revisited that day and felt again the frustration and the desire to be the first to discover the egg's secret. However, looking with understanding and forgiveness, they realized that they both shared the same passion and could have explored together.

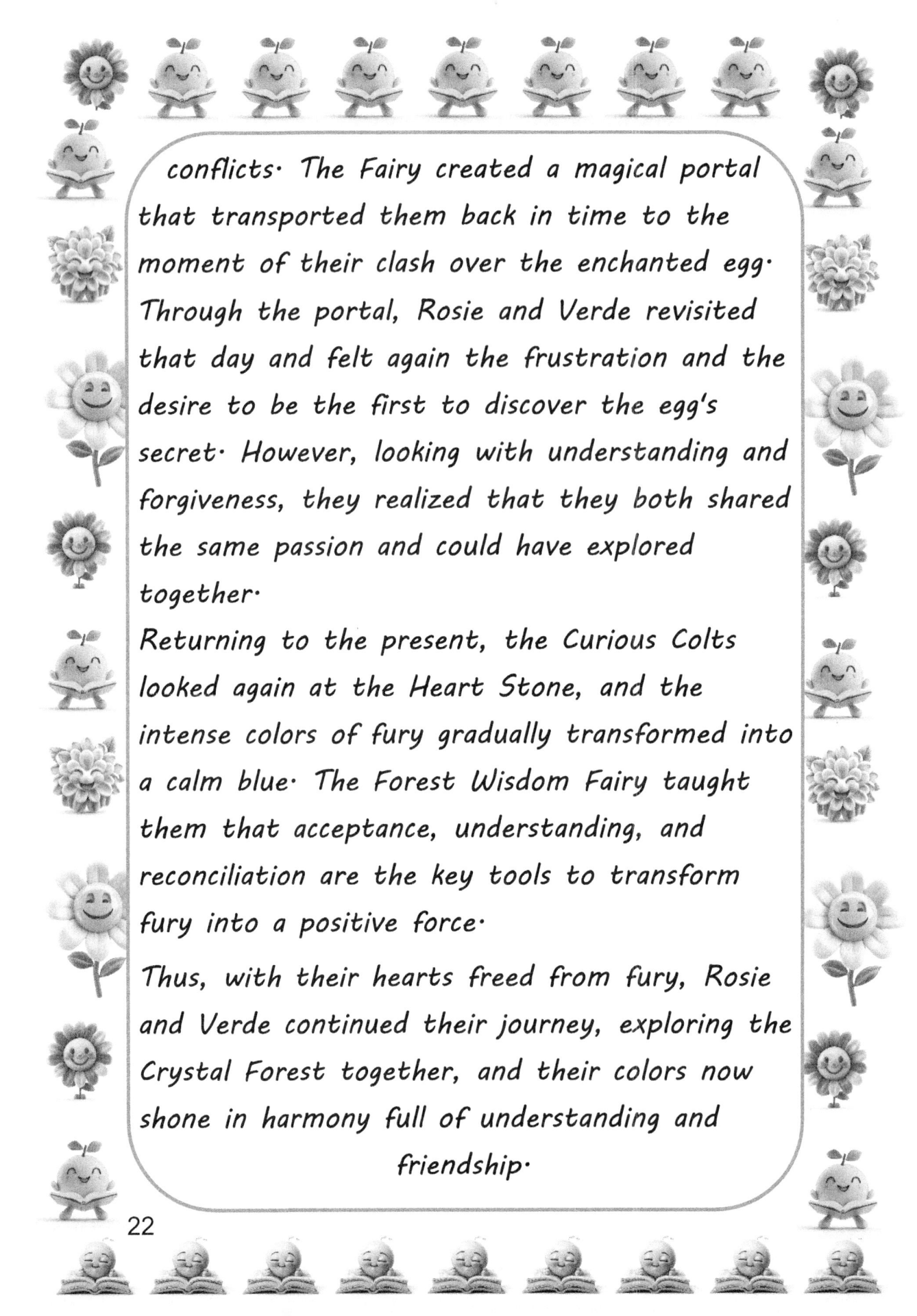

Returning to the present, the Curious Colts looked again at the Heart Stone, and the intense colors of fury gradually transformed into a calm blue. The Forest Wisdom Fairy taught them that acceptance, understanding, and reconciliation are the key tools to transform fury into a positive force.

Thus, with their hearts freed from fury, Rosie and Verde continued their journey, exploring the Crystal Forest together, and their colors now shone in harmony full of understanding and friendship.

Fear

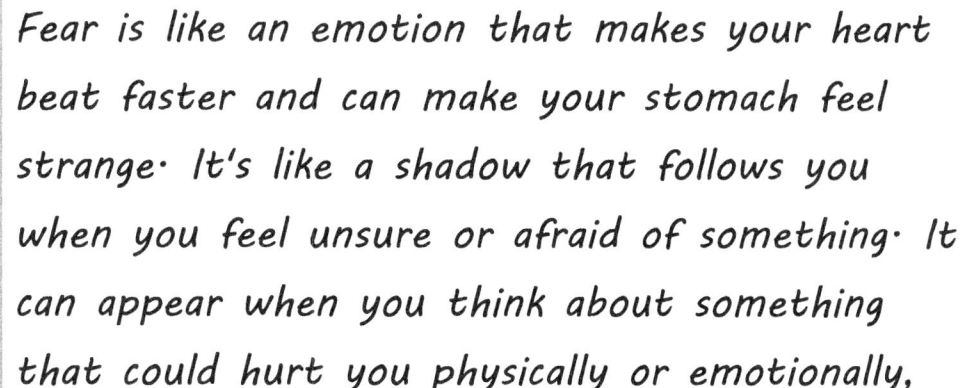

Fear is like an emotion that makes your heart beat faster and can make your stomach feel strange. It's like a shadow that follows you when you feel unsure or afraid of something. It can appear when you think about something that could hurt you physically or emotionally, or when you're confronted with something unknown.

When we're scared, our bodies react in different ways. For example, the heart starts beating faster to prepare us to face the situation of danger. Breathing can become faster and shallower. Our muscles can tense up, preparing for action or reacting to stress. Sometimes, we may feel sweaty or shaky.

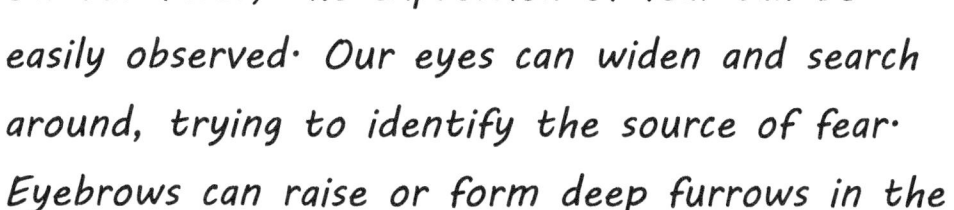

On our faces, the expression of fear can be easily observed. Our eyes can widen and search around, trying to identify the source of fear. Eyebrows can raise or form deep furrows in the forehead. The mouth can be tightened or slightly open, and the lips can become paler or tighter. All these signs can help us recognize when someone is scared or when we ourselves are.

Regarding body language, it's important to observe how we react when we feel scared. We may pull back, cover our face, or cross our arms, as if trying to protect ourselves from something. In some cases, we may have the tendency to move away from situations that cause us fear, or we may seek support and safety from our loved ones.

Fear can be an overwhelming experience, but it's important to remember that it's a normal emotion and that we can learn to manage it. We can do this by practicing deep breathing techniques, thinking of solutions to our problems, and seeking support and understanding in our community.

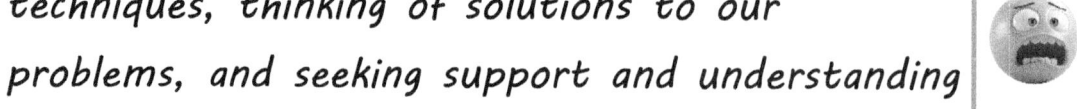

So, my dear friends, let's not forget that fear can be faced and managed with courage and mutual support. Let's stand by each other in the face of our fears and seek light even in the darkest moments!

Here are some tips that might help you.

Draw your fears: Take paper and colored pencils and draw what scares you. Then, turn the image into something funny or amusing. For example, if you're afraid of monsters, draw them as funny creatures.

Butterfly breath: Imagine you're butterflies and take slow, deep breaths, inflating and deflating your "wings" (chest) like butterflies. This can help you feel calmer.

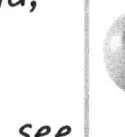

Seek the light: At night, when you feel afraid, turn on a night light or ask your parents to leave the door slightly open. Light helps you see that there are no monsters in the room.

Make yourself a superhero mask: Create your own superhero masks out of paper and wear them when you feel afraid. You'll instantly become stronger and braver.

Invent stories of courage: Write or tell stories about the times when you're super brave. These stories will help you feel stronger and overcome your fears.

Share with someone: If you're feeling scared, talk to your parents, grandparents, or friends about it. Sometimes, talking about what scares you will make you feel better.

Play with stuffed animals: Do you have a favorite stuffed toy? Take it with you when you feel scared. A stuffed toy can bring comfort and security.

Dance to your favorite tunes: Put on music and dance in your room when you feel scared. Movement and music can make you feel happier and stronger.

Create a courage box: Decorate a small box and put drawings, stories, or objects that bring you courage inside. When you feel scared, open the box and find courage inside.

Yoga exercises for kids: Try special yoga exercises for kids that can help you relax and feel more connected to your body. There are many videos and books on this subject that you can explore with your parents or friends.

Plan a courage party: Organize a themed party to celebrate courage and encourage each other to share moments when you've been brave. You can decorate together and enjoy snacks and fun games.

Exploration expeditions: Organize exploration expeditions in the backyard or nearby park, looking for hidden treasures or interesting things. Exploring nature can help you feel more confident and focus on the beautiful things around you.

Journeys in imagination: Use your imagination to travel to fantastic places and imagine facing fear in the boldest ways possible. Create your own adventures and explore new territories in your mind.

Role-playing games: Play role-playing games where you become brave characters and face various challenges or obstacles. This can help you develop your imagination and feel stronger in the face of your fears.

Happy ending movie nights: Organize movie nights with inspiring stories or happy endings that offer you a dose of optimism and courage. Discuss the positive messages from the movies and how the characters handle fear and challenges.

So, dear friends, don't forget that each of you is a little hero and that you have the power to overcome your fears. Be brave and don't hesitate to seek help from the adults around you.

Journey of Spark and the Light of Friendship

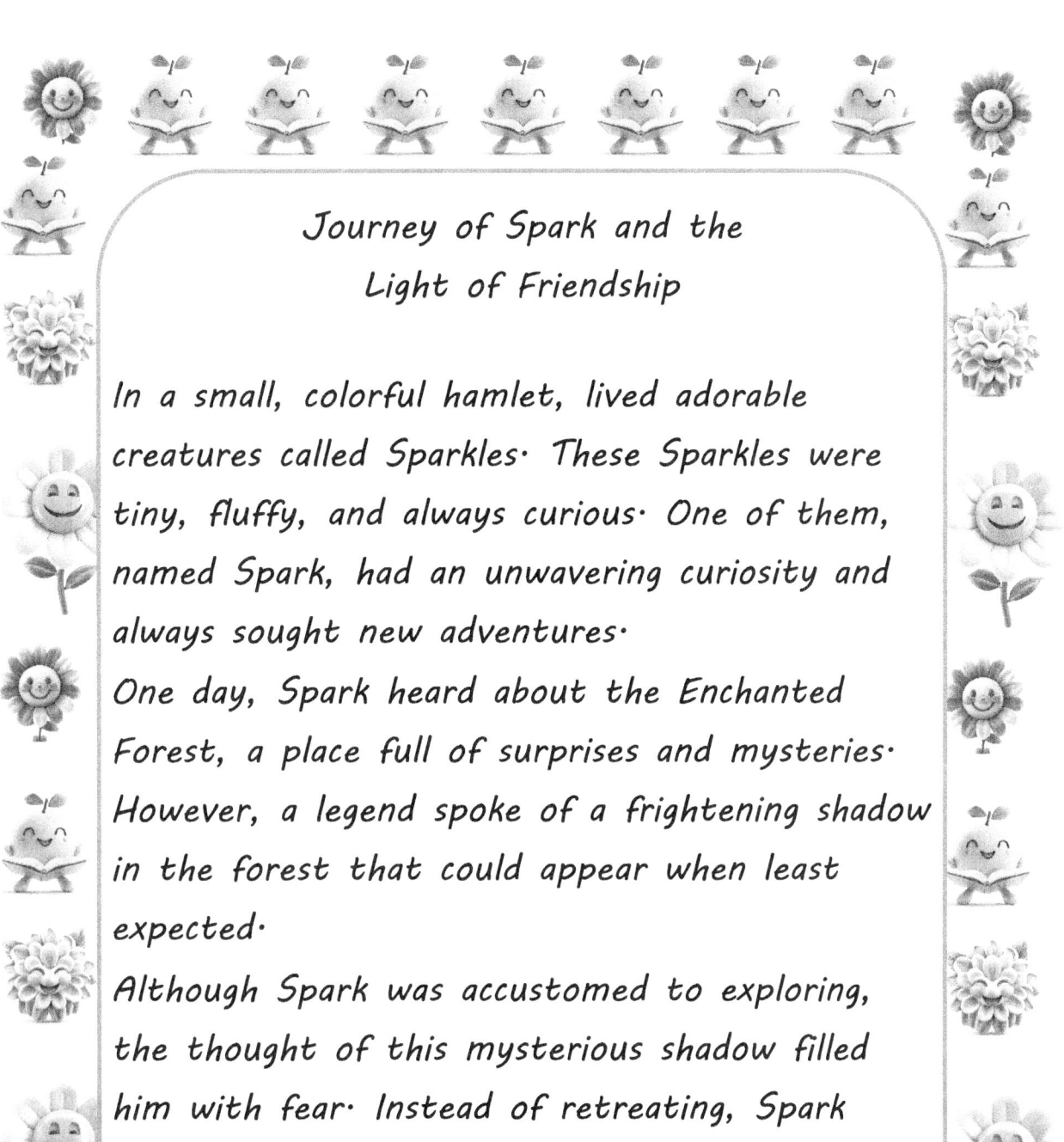

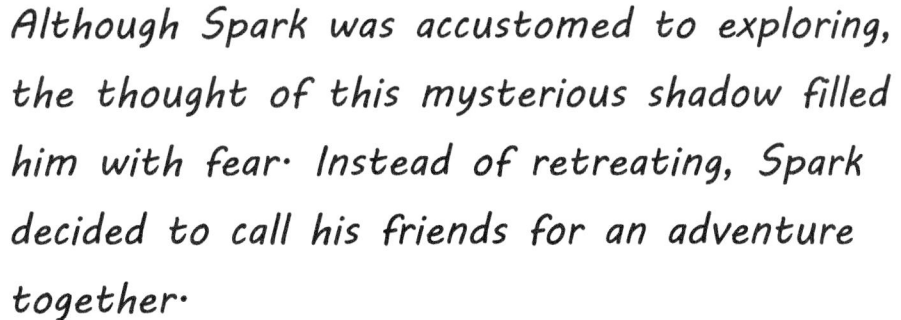

In a small, colorful hamlet, lived adorable creatures called Sparkles. These Sparkles were tiny, fluffy, and always curious. One of them, named Spark, had an unwavering curiosity and always sought new adventures.

One day, Spark heard about the Enchanted Forest, a place full of surprises and mysteries. However, a legend spoke of a frightening shadow in the forest that could appear when least expected.

Although Spark was accustomed to exploring, the thought of this mysterious shadow filled him with fear. Instead of retreating, Spark decided to call his friends for an adventure together.

Alongside Flare, Grinny, and Puff, Spark embarked on the journey to the Enchanted Forest. With each step, the trees rose like colorful towers, and the cheerful sound of birds encouraged their courage.

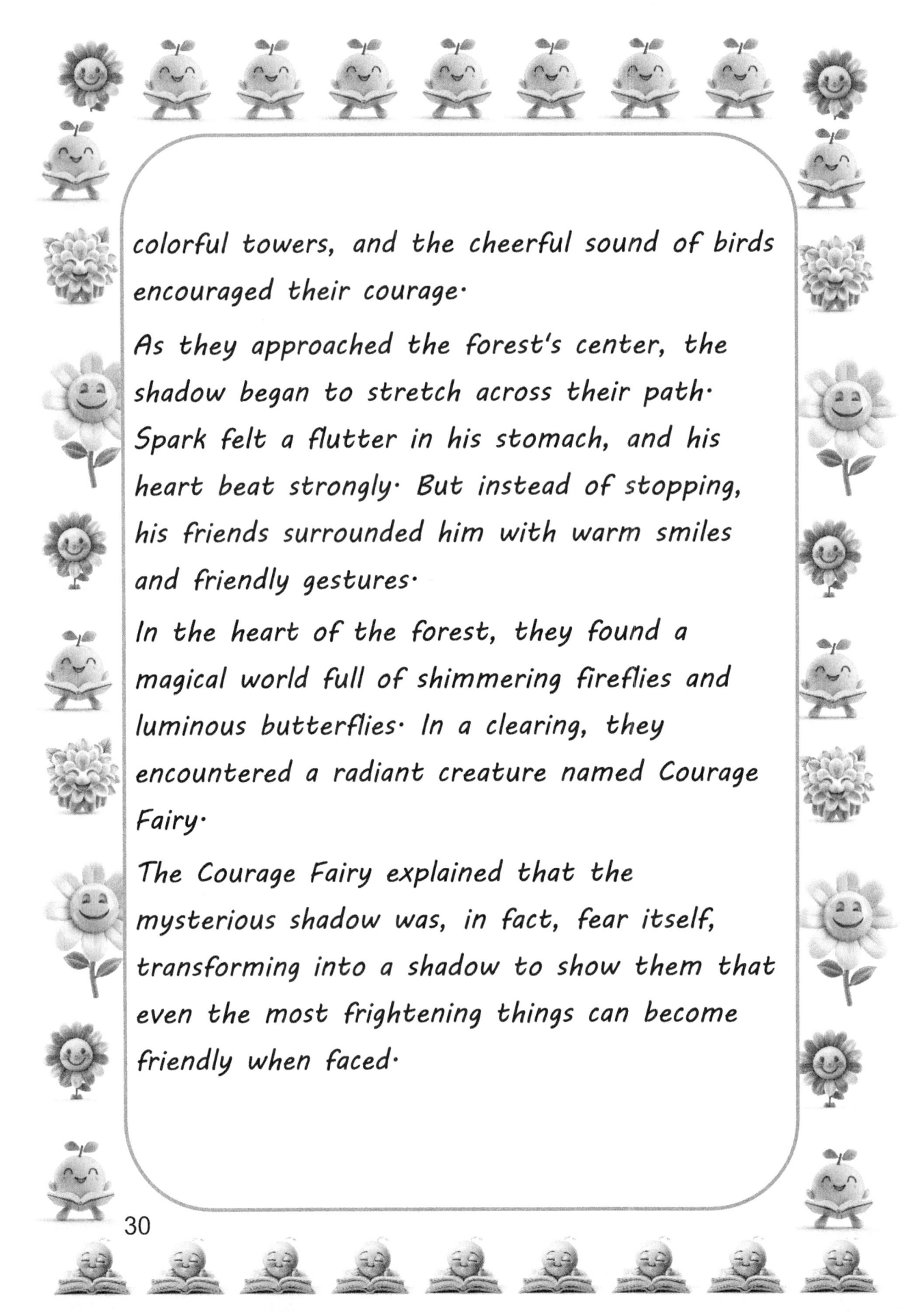

As they approached the forest's center, the shadow began to stretch across their path. Spark felt a flutter in his stomach, and his heart beat strongly. But instead of stopping, his friends surrounded him with warm smiles and friendly gestures.

In the heart of the forest, they found a magical world full of shimmering fireflies and luminous butterflies. In a clearing, they encountered a radiant creature named Courage Fairy.

The Courage Fairy explained that the mysterious shadow was, in fact, fear itself, transforming into a shadow to show them that even the most frightening things can become friendly when faced.

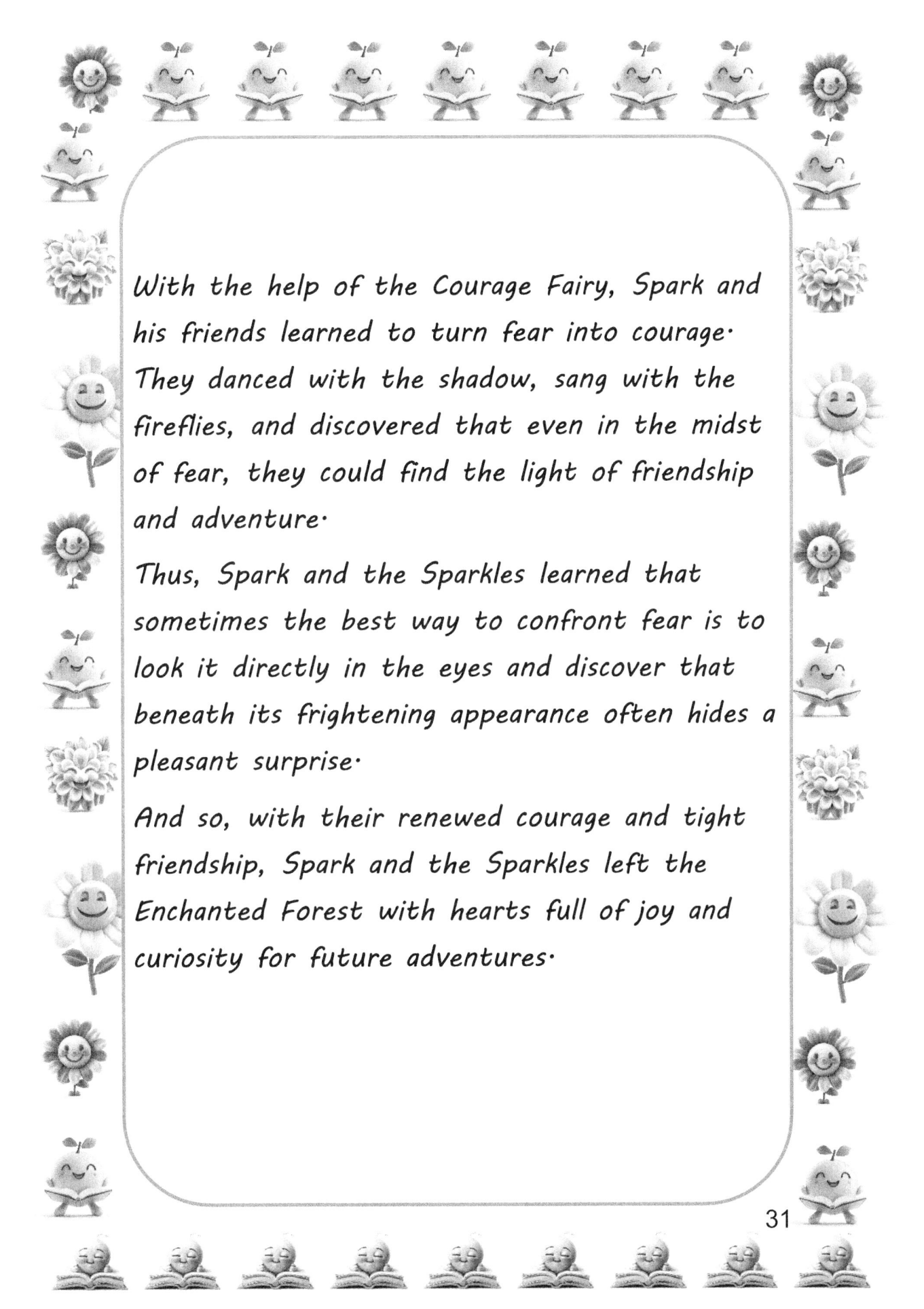

With the help of the Courage Fairy, Spark and his friends learned to turn fear into courage. They danced with the shadow, sang with the fireflies, and discovered that even in the midst of fear, they could find the light of friendship and adventure.

Thus, Spark and the Sparkles learned that sometimes the best way to confront fear is to look it directly in the eyes and discover that beneath its frightening appearance often hides a pleasant surprise.

And so, with their renewed courage and tight friendship, Spark and the Sparkles left the Enchanted Forest with hearts full of joy and curiosity for future adventures.

Disgust

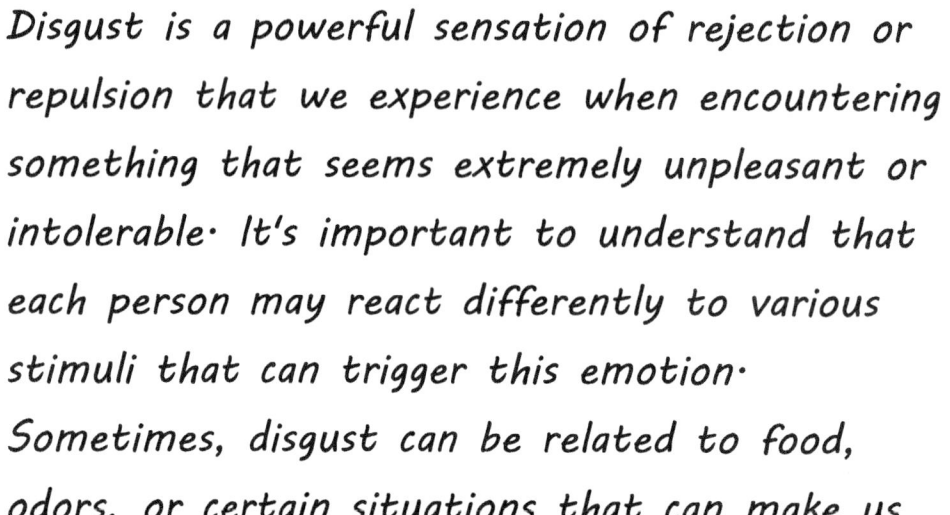

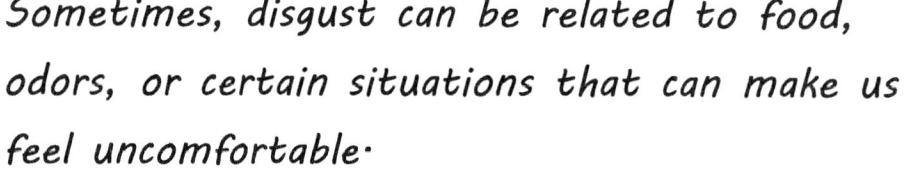

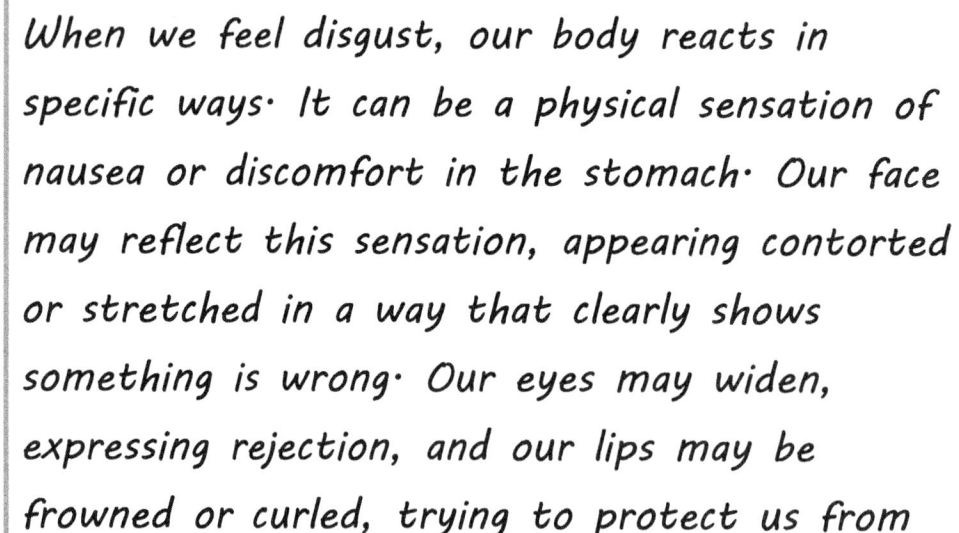

Disgust is a powerful sensation of rejection or repulsion that we experience when encountering something that seems extremely unpleasant or intolerable. It's important to understand that each person may react differently to various stimuli that can trigger this emotion. Sometimes, disgust can be related to food, odors, or certain situations that can make us feel uncomfortable.

When we feel disgust, our body reacts in specific ways. It can be a physical sensation of nausea or discomfort in the stomach. Our face may reflect this sensation, appearing contorted or stretched in a way that clearly shows something is wrong. Our eyes may widen, expressing rejection, and our lips may be frowned or curled, trying to protect us from something we perceive as bad.

In addition to facial expressions, body language can also speak about disgust. We may physically distance ourselves from the object or situation that bothers us, we may have a reflex to cover our mouth or nose with our hand, or we may even withdraw or move away from what provokes this emotion.

Sense of taste and smell: Disgust can be triggered by certain aromas or tastes that seem unpleasant or even disgusting. For example, the taste of a dish we don't like or the strong smell of a cleaning product can provoke this emotion.

Tactile sense: Sometimes, touching an object or a substance can trigger disgust. If we touch something wet, sticky, or slimy, it may be enough to provoke this reaction.

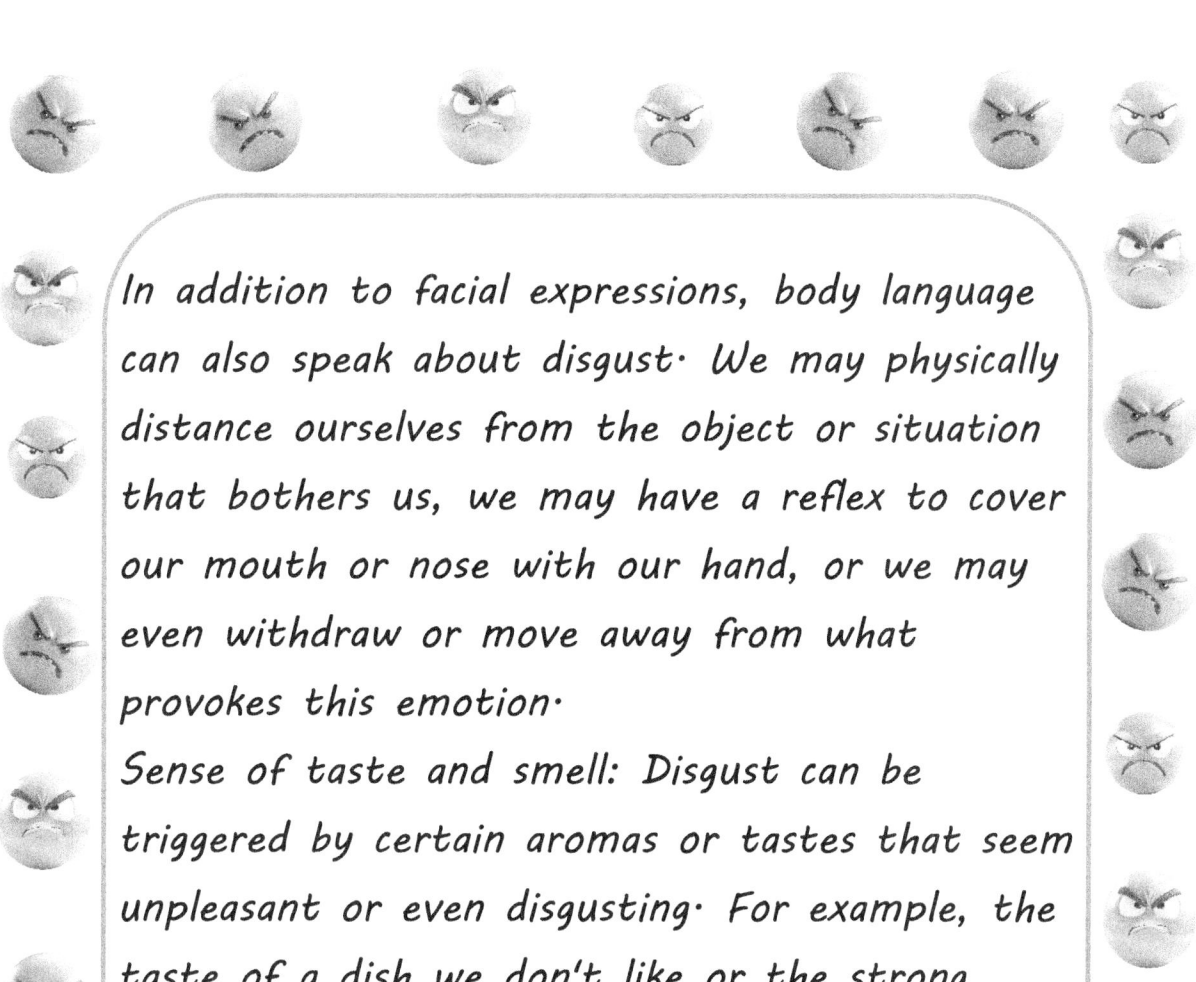

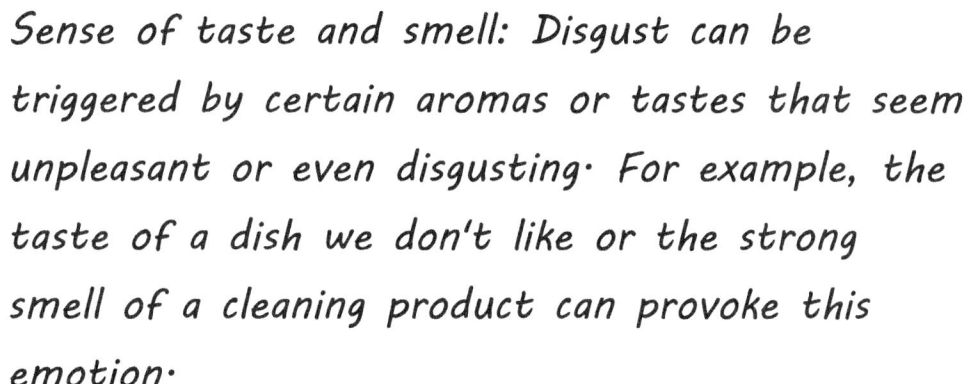

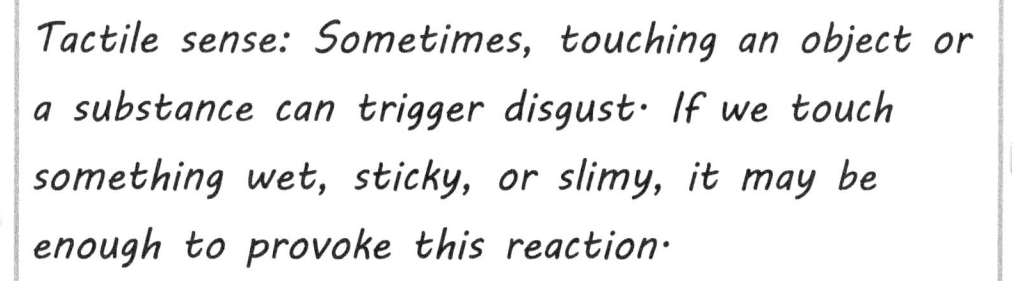

Visual aspect: The visual aspect of an object or situation can also be a major factor in triggering the emotion of disgust. If we see something dirty, decomposed, or that seems dangerous, we can experience this sensation.

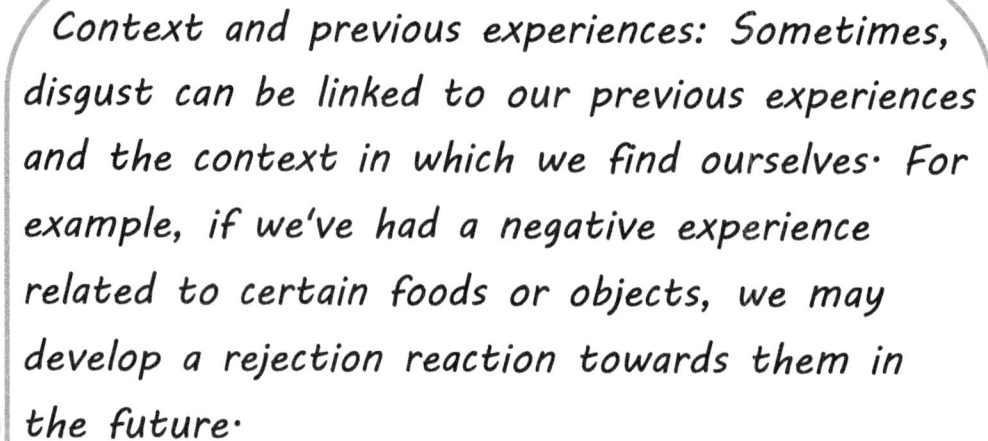

Context and previous experiences: Sometimes, disgust can be linked to our previous experiences and the context in which we find ourselves. For example, if we've had a negative experience related to certain foods or objects, we may develop a rejection reaction towards them in the future.

Physical and behavioral reactions: When we feel disgust, our body can react in various ways. We may have a feeling of nausea in the stomach, we may feel weak, or we may physically withdraw from the object that bothers us. Our gestures may include frowning, closing our eyes, or even moving our hand away from a disgusting object.

In conclusion, disgust is a complex reaction that can be triggered by multiple factors and can vary from one person to another. It's important to be aware of this emotion and learn to manage it in healthy and respectful ways. By understanding and accepting our emotions, we can develop important self-regulation skills and empathy towards others.

Here are some tips for managing feelings of disgust

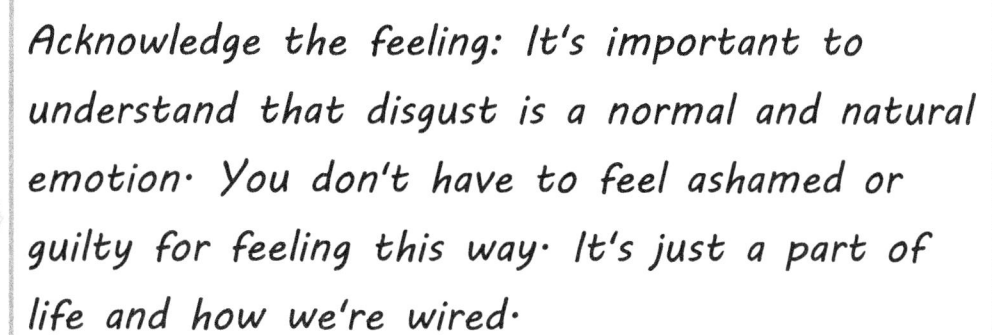

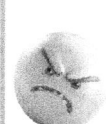

Acknowledge the feeling: It's important to understand that disgust is a normal and natural emotion. You don't have to feel ashamed or guilty for feeling this way. It's just a part of life and how we're wired.

Express your emotions: Don't be afraid to talk about what makes you feel disgusted. You can talk to your parents, friends, or a trusted adult. By talking about your feelings, you'll find that you're not alone and that others may have similar experiences.

Identify the sources of disgust: Try to identify what specifically is making you feel this way. It's important to understand why you feel disgusted so you can find solutions to deal with these situations.

Avoid sources of disgust if possible: If you know that certain things or situations make you feel disgusted, try to avoid them as much as possible. For example, if certain foods or smells make you feel sick, try to stay away from them.

Think about solutions: If there are situations you can't avoid, think about ways to cope with them. Sharing your feelings with someone or finding strategies to minimize the impact of disgust may help you feel better.

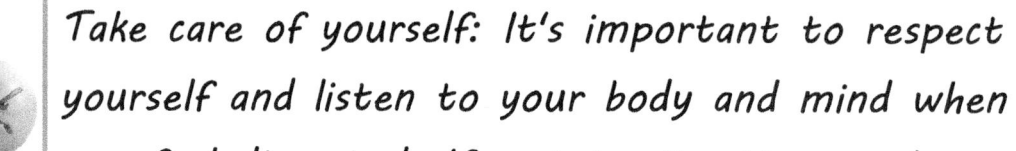

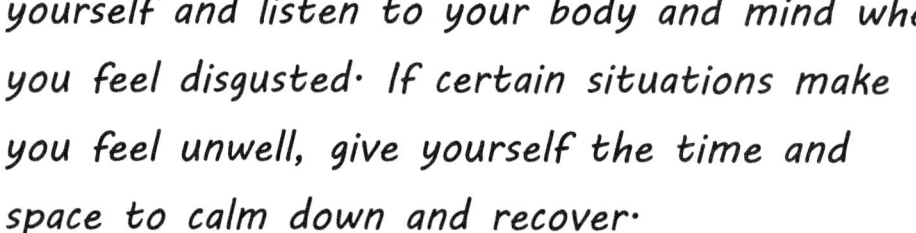

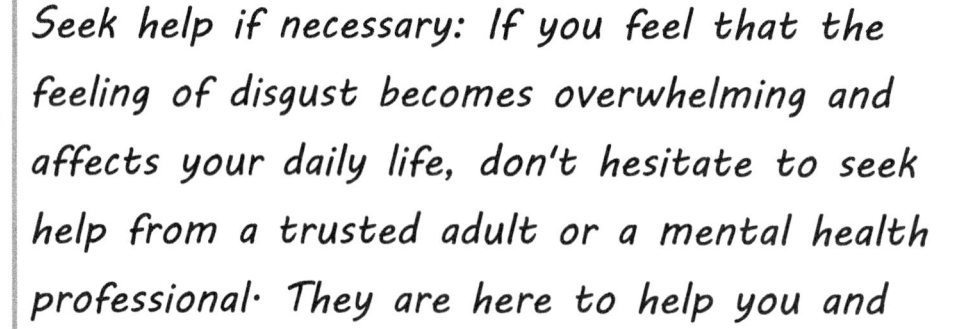

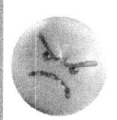

Take care of yourself: It's important to respect yourself and listen to your body and mind when you feel disgusted. If certain situations make you feel unwell, give yourself the time and space to calm down and recover.

Seek help if necessary: If you feel that the feeling of disgust becomes overwhelming and affects your daily life, don't hesitate to seek help from a trusted adult or a mental health professional. They are here to help you and provide the support you need to cope with these emotions.

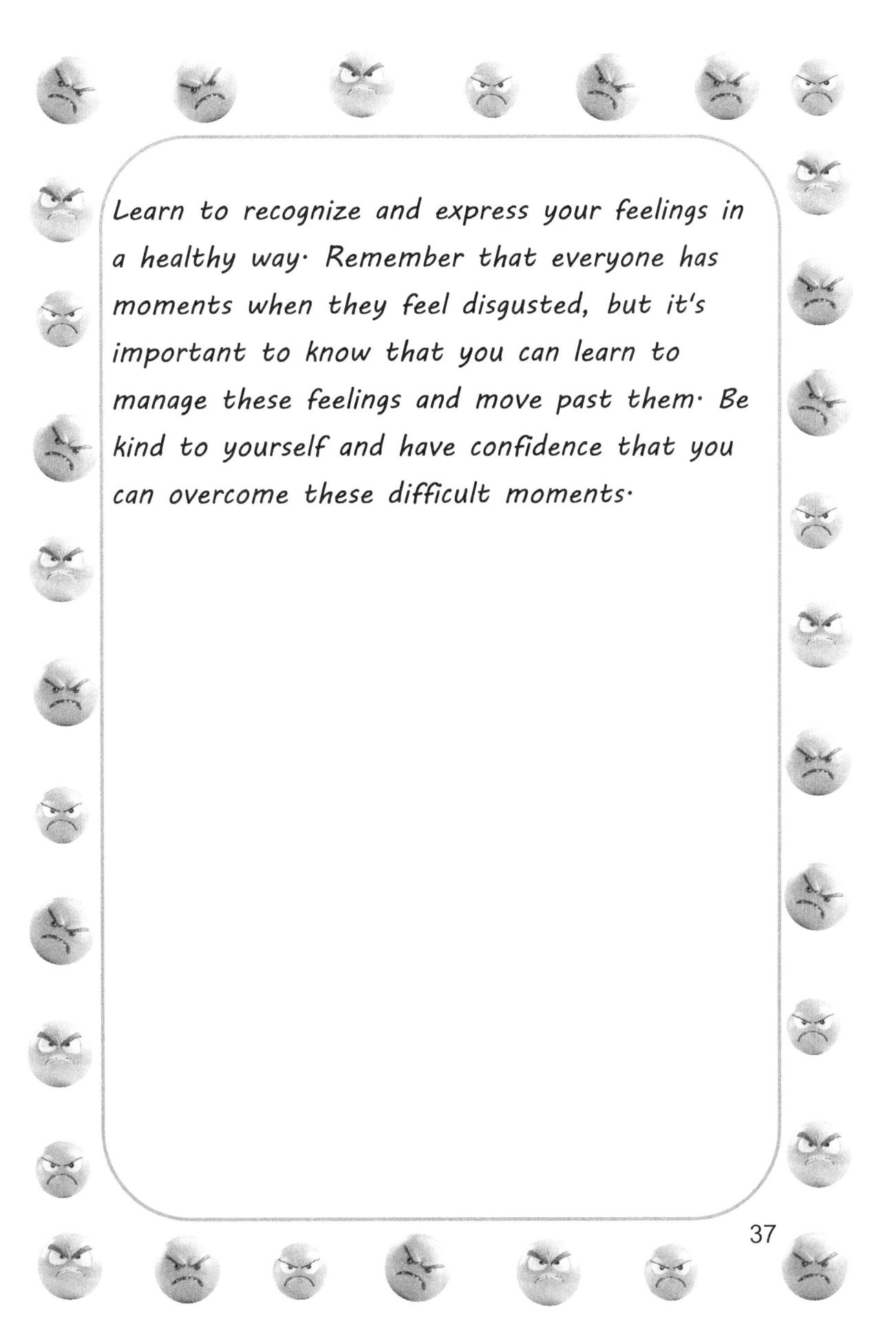

Learn to recognize and express your feelings in a healthy way. Remember that everyone has moments when they feel disgusted, but it's important to know that you can learn to manage these feelings and move past them. Be kind to yourself and have confidence that you can overcome these difficult moments.

Luca's Story

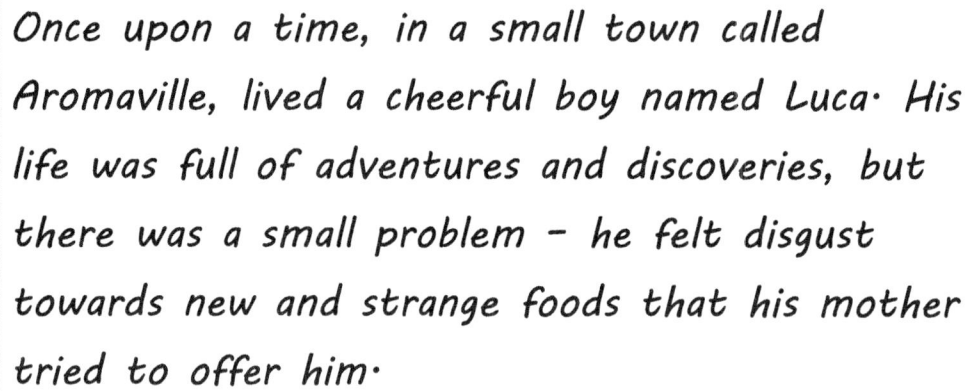

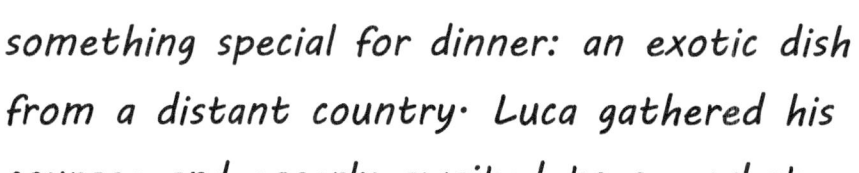

Once upon a time, in a small town called Aromaville, lived a cheerful boy named Luca. His life was full of adventures and discoveries, but there was a small problem – he felt disgust towards new and strange foods that his mother tried to offer him.

One day, Luca's mother decided to try something special for dinner: an exotic dish from a distant country. Luca gathered his courage and eagerly awaited to see what surprise awaited him. However, when he looked at the plate filled with unfamiliar aromas, his facial expression turned into one of disgust.

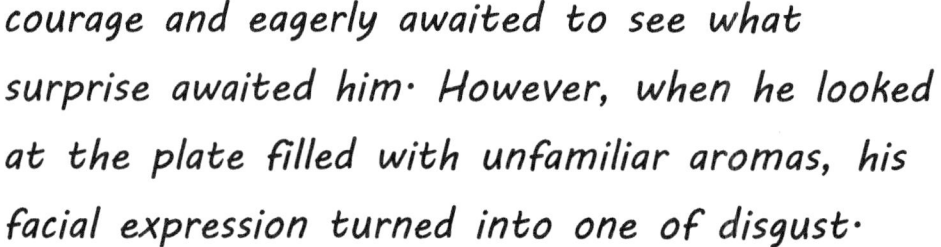

"What is this, Mom?" exclaimed Luca, biting timidly into the food.

His mother leaned down with a smile and said, "It's a secret recipe from the land of kitchen fairies. It might seem strange at first, but who knows, maybe you'll like it!"

Luca, although skeptical, decided to try to overcome the unusual taste. Despite his efforts, he couldn't hide the look of disgust.

Concerned for her son, Luca's mother decided to turn this experience into an adventure. She brought colorful plates, shiny forks, and set up a festive table. "Luca, let's try to turn this dinner into a taste party!"

Luca looked amazed and, encouraged by his mother's cheerful attitude, began to explore the unique flavors of the dishes. They invented funny games where they had to guess the ingredients and gave each other ratings for creativity.

While having fun, Luca and his mother discovered that disgust had turned into an adventure full of laughter and discoveries. They enjoyed every taste and learned to appreciate the diversity of world cuisines.

Since then, Luca no longer felt disgust towards new foods. He became a little explorer of

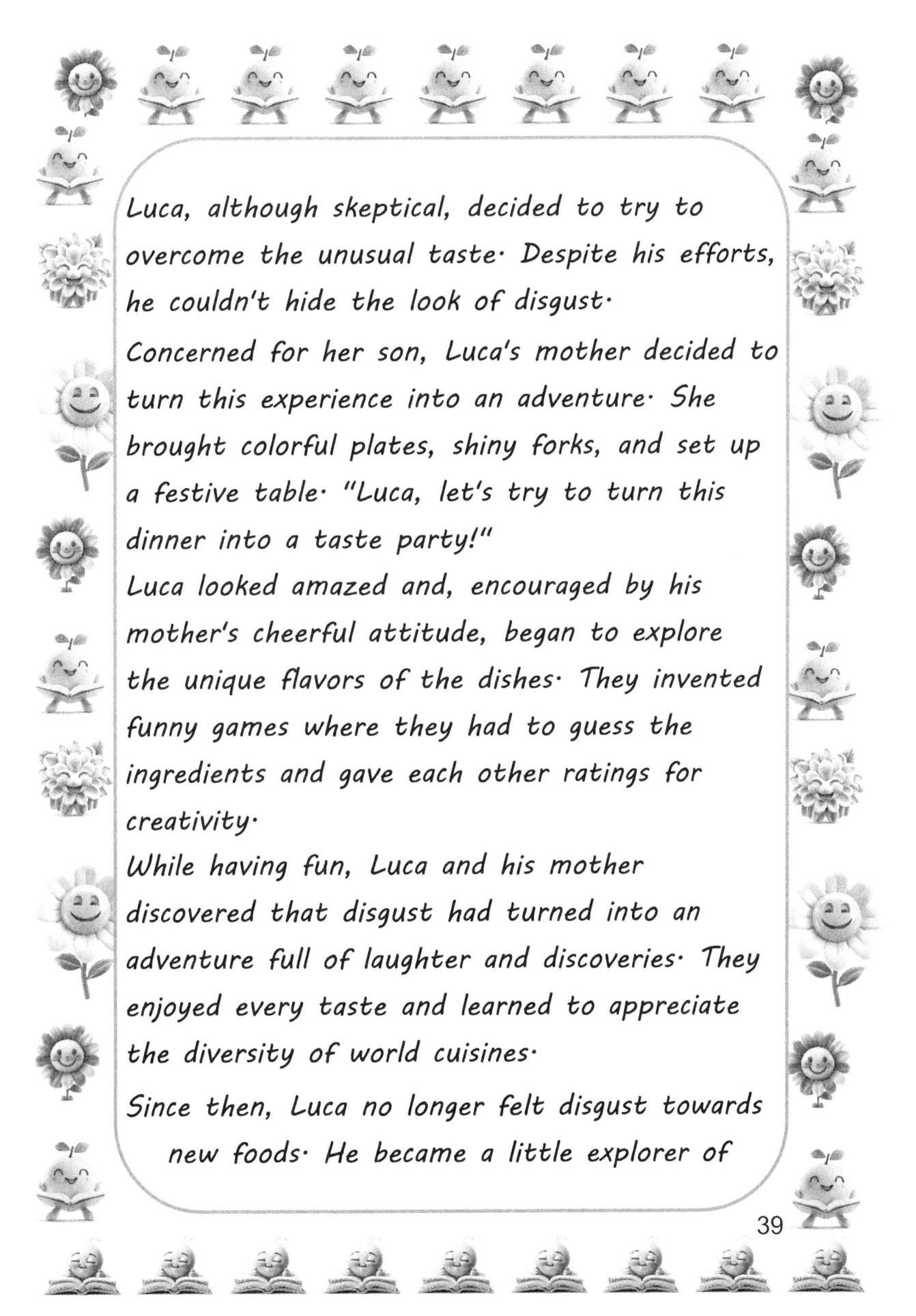

kitchens, sharing his experiences with all his friends. In Aromaville, every dinner was now a taste party, where all the children learned to appreciate and love culinary diversity.

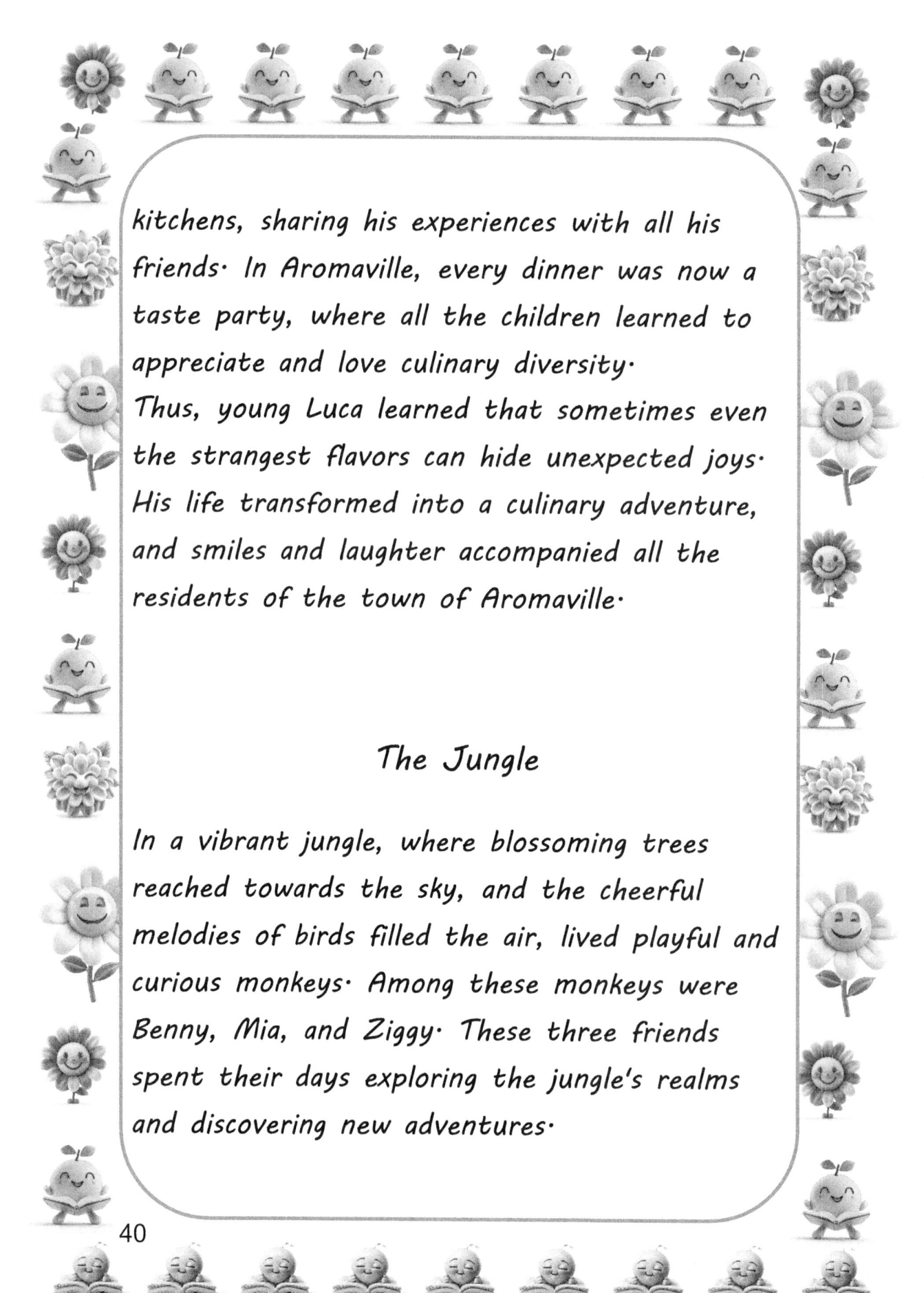

Thus, young Luca learned that sometimes even the strangest flavors can hide unexpected joys. His life transformed into a culinary adventure, and smiles and laughter accompanied all the residents of the town of Aromaville.

The Jungle

In a vibrant jungle, where blossoming trees reached towards the sky, and the cheerful melodies of birds filled the air, lived playful and curious monkeys. Among these monkeys were Benny, Mia, and Ziggy. These three friends spent their days exploring the jungle's realms and discovering new adventures.

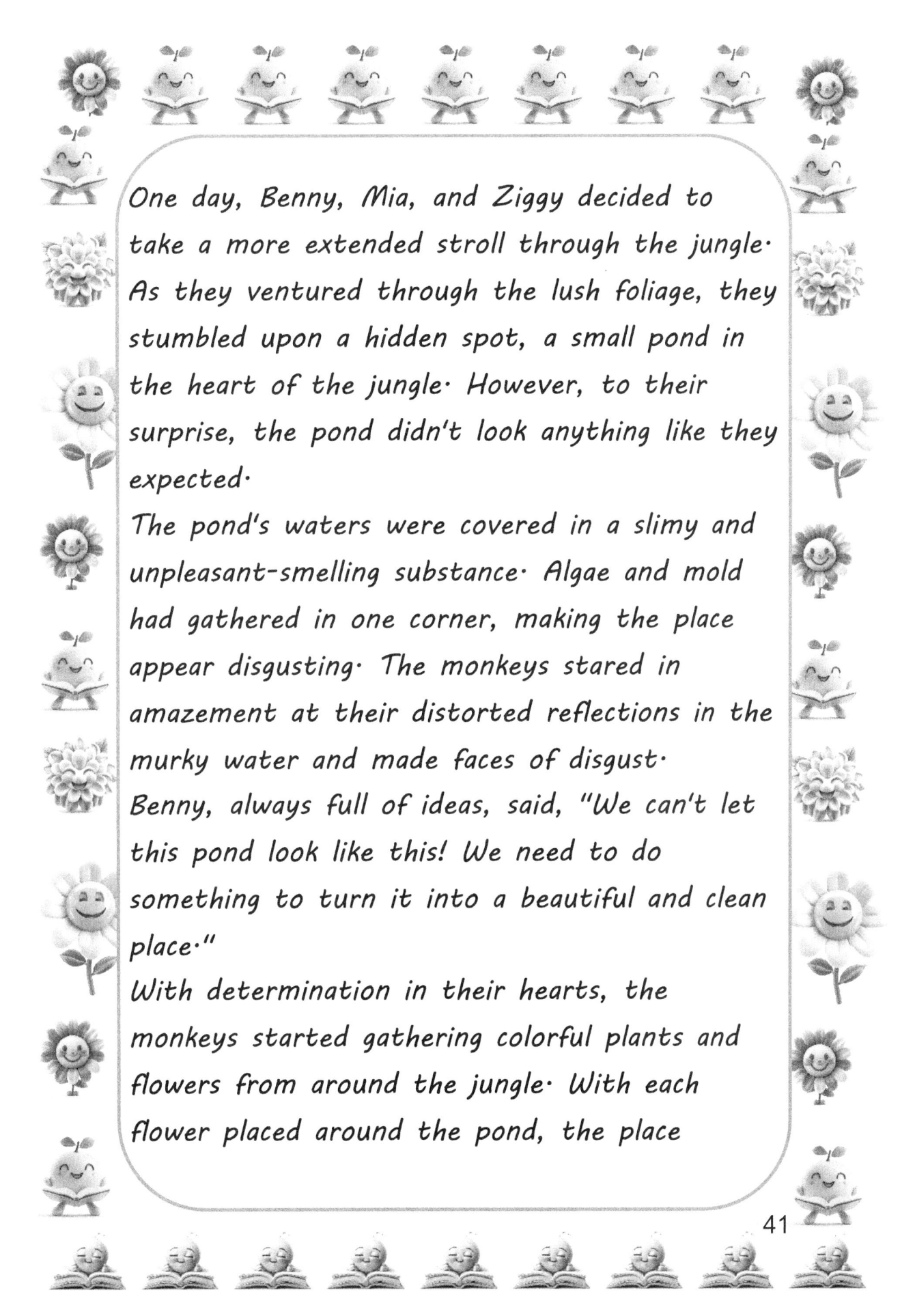

One day, Benny, Mia, and Ziggy decided to take a more extended stroll through the jungle. As they ventured through the lush foliage, they stumbled upon a hidden spot, a small pond in the heart of the jungle. However, to their surprise, the pond didn't look anything like they expected.

The pond's waters were covered in a slimy and unpleasant-smelling substance. Algae and mold had gathered in one corner, making the place appear disgusting. The monkeys stared in amazement at their distorted reflections in the murky water and made faces of disgust.

Benny, always full of ideas, said, "We can't let this pond look like this! We need to do something to turn it into a beautiful and clean place."

With determination in their hearts, the monkeys started gathering colorful plants and flowers from around the jungle. With each flower placed around the pond, the place seemed to come to life and breathe again. As they worked, the monkeys laughed and sang, and the previously disgusting atmosphere gradually disappeared.

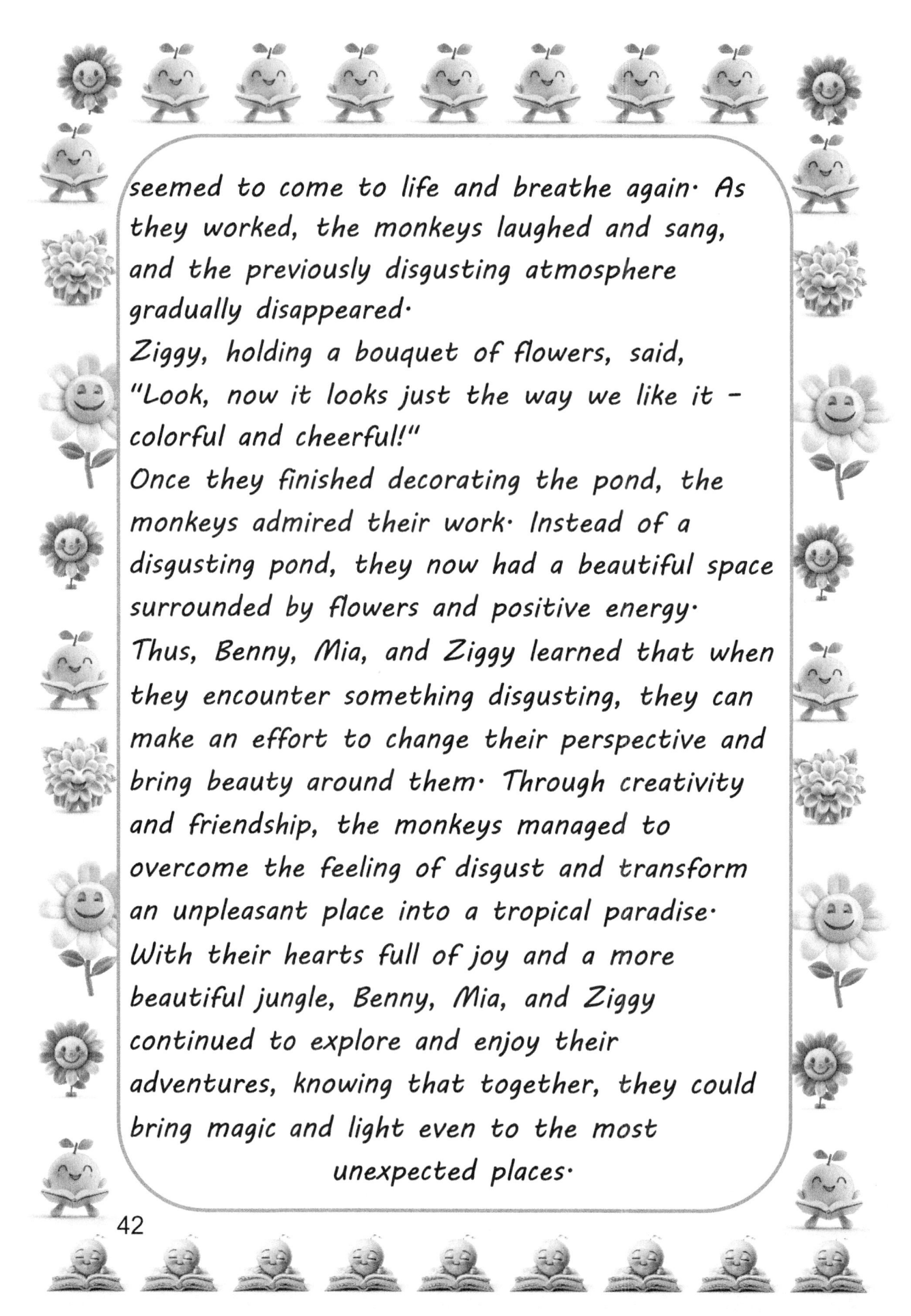

Ziggy, holding a bouquet of flowers, said, "Look, now it looks just the way we like it - colorful and cheerful!"

Once they finished decorating the pond, the monkeys admired their work. Instead of a disgusting pond, they now had a beautiful space surrounded by flowers and positive energy.

Thus, Benny, Mia, and Ziggy learned that when they encounter something disgusting, they can make an effort to change their perspective and bring beauty around them. Through creativity and friendship, the monkeys managed to overcome the feeling of disgust and transform an unpleasant place into a tropical paradise. With their hearts full of joy and a more beautiful jungle, Benny, Mia, and Ziggy continued to explore and enjoy their adventures, knowing that together, they could bring magic and light even to the most unexpected places.

Emotion of Surprise

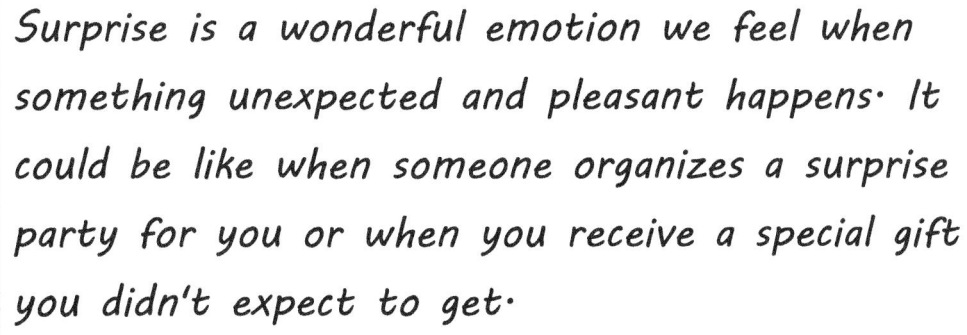

Surprise is a wonderful emotion we feel when something unexpected and pleasant happens. It could be like when someone organizes a surprise party for you or when you receive a special gift you didn't expect to get.

When we experience surprise, our face lights up with amazement and joy. Our eyes widen, our mouth may open into a huge smile, and our eyebrows rise. It's like we're saying "WOW!" with our whole face.

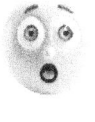

Apart from the facial expression, our body can also show surprise. We might freeze in place, waiting to see what happens next, or we might jiggle with joy, jump up and down, and move quickly.

What makes surprise so special is that it makes us feel an emotion full of energy and anticipation. It's like a little burst of happiness in our hearts, making us feel alive and vibrating with excitement.

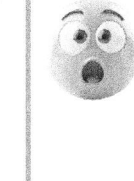

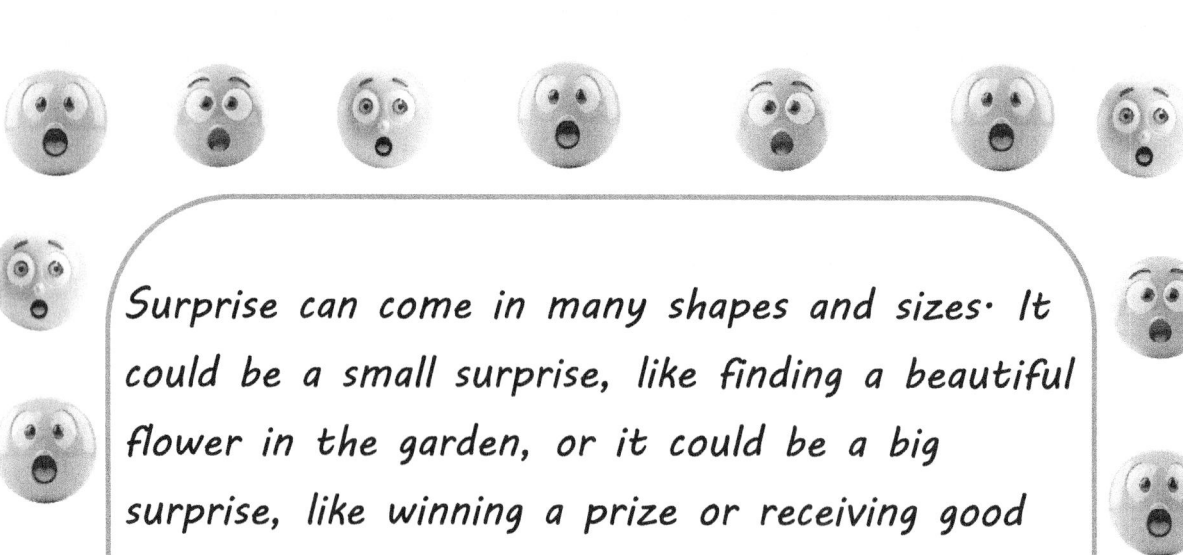

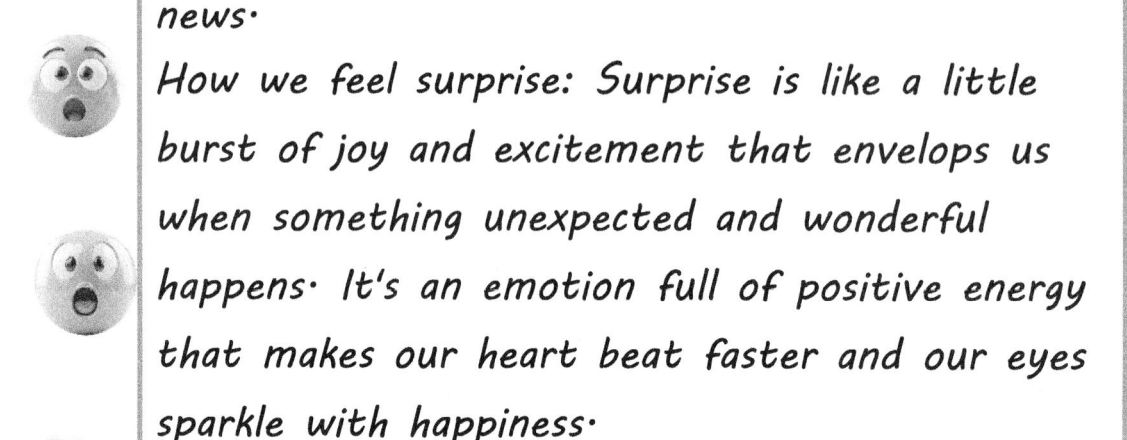

Surprise can come in many shapes and sizes. It could be a small surprise, like finding a beautiful flower in the garden, or it could be a big surprise, like winning a prize or receiving good news.

How we feel surprise: Surprise is like a little burst of joy and excitement that envelops us when something unexpected and wonderful happens. It's an emotion full of positive energy that makes our heart beat faster and our eyes sparkle with happiness.

How it looks on our face: When we're surprised, our eyes become wide and bright, our mouth opens into a wide smile, and our eyebrows rise in astonishment. Our face shines with happiness and amazement, and this can be seen in our expression.

How we recognize surprise: We realize we're surprised when we feel a flutter of emotion in our stomach, and our heart starts to beat *faster. Our eyes lock onto the thing or event that surprised us, and a smile appears on our face without us realizing it.*

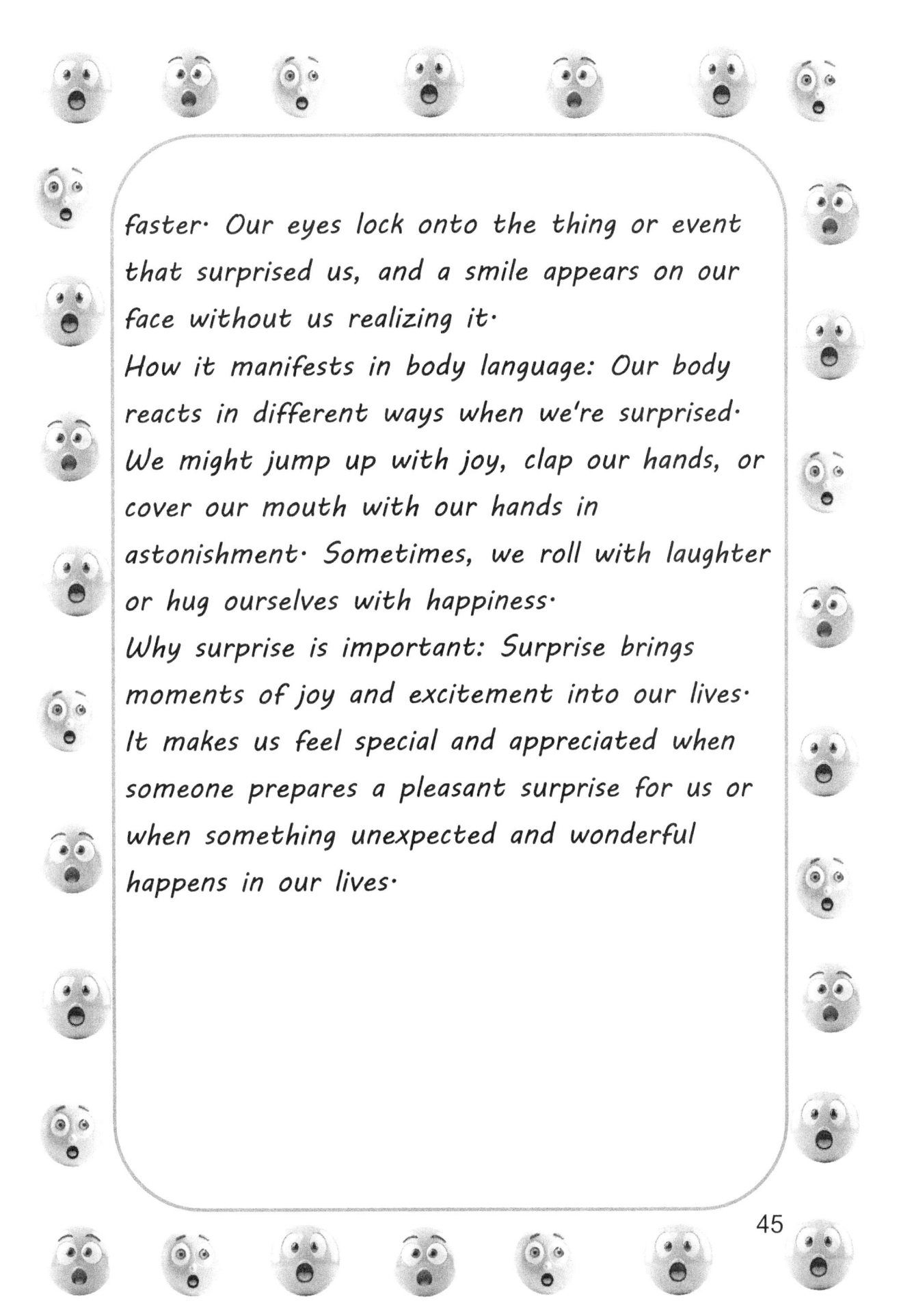

How it manifests in body language: Our body reacts in different ways when we're surprised. We might jump up with joy, clap our hands, or cover our mouth with our hands in astonishment. Sometimes, we roll with laughter or hug ourselves with happiness.

Why surprise is important: Surprise brings moments of joy and excitement into our lives. It makes us feel special and appreciated when someone prepares a pleasant surprise for us or when something unexpected and wonderful happens in our lives.

A Day Full of Surprises in the Land of Smiles

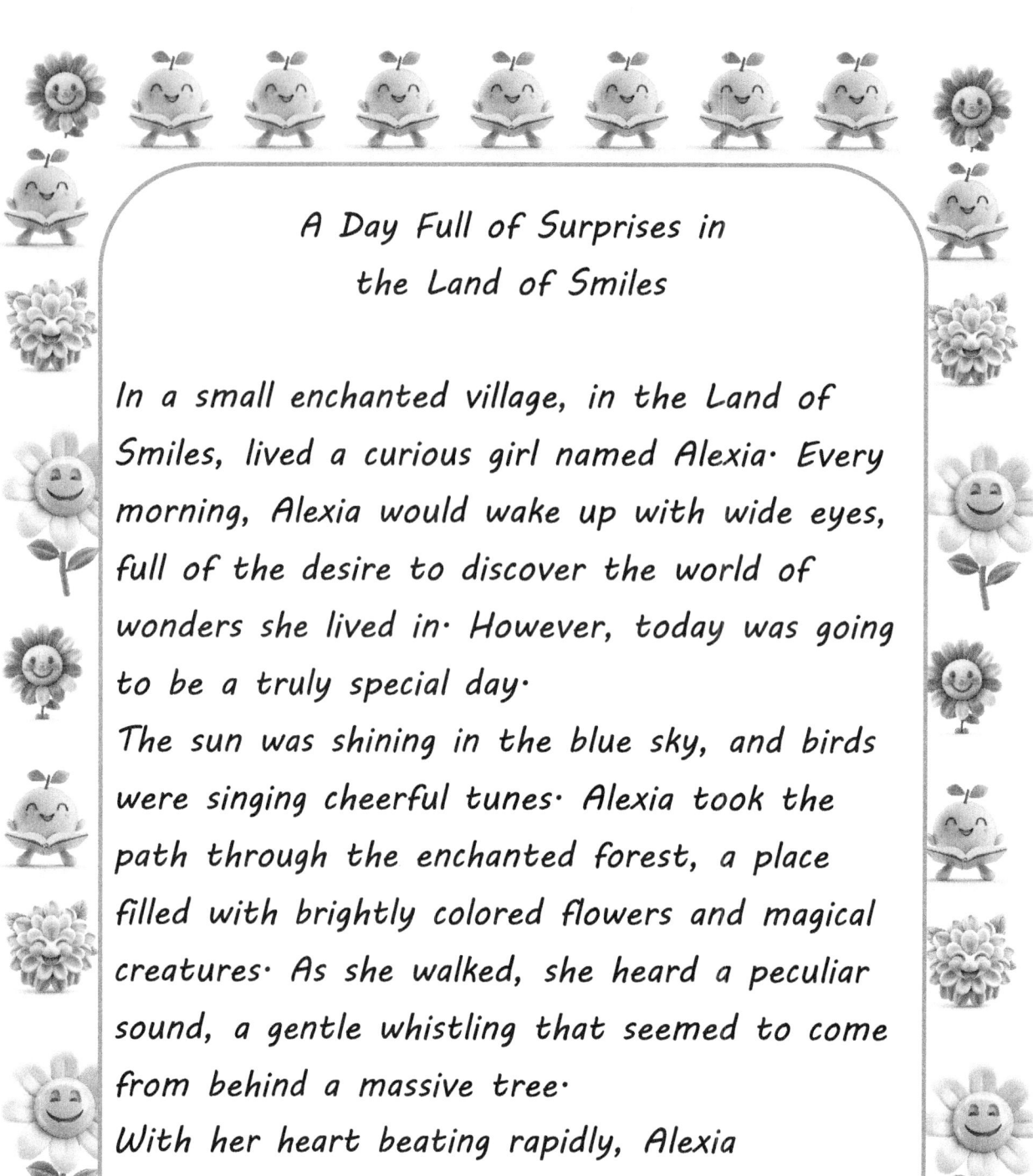

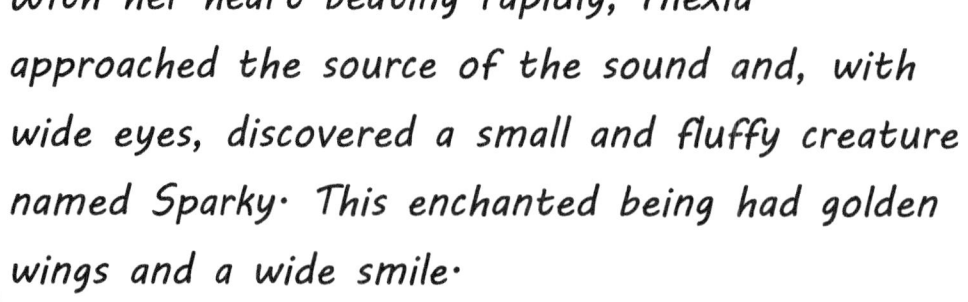

In a small enchanted village, in the Land of Smiles, lived a curious girl named Alexia. Every morning, Alexia would wake up with wide eyes, full of the desire to discover the world of wonders she lived in. However, today was going to be a truly special day.

The sun was shining in the blue sky, and birds were singing cheerful tunes. Alexia took the path through the enchanted forest, a place filled with brightly colored flowers and magical creatures. As she walked, she heard a peculiar sound, a gentle whistling that seemed to come from behind a massive tree.

With her heart beating rapidly, Alexia approached the source of the sound and, with wide eyes, discovered a small and fluffy creature named Sparky. This enchanted being had golden wings and a wide smile.

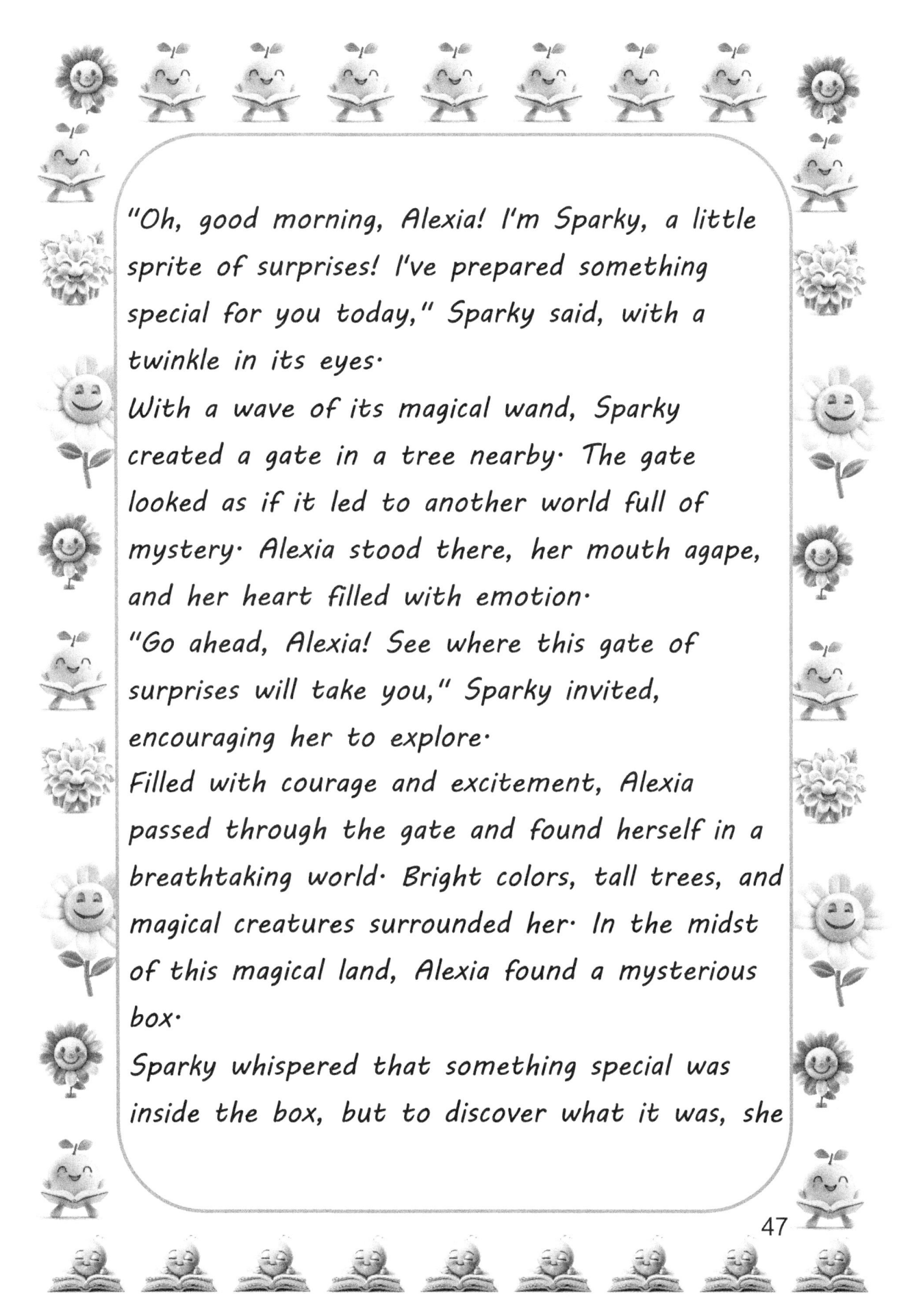

"Oh, good morning, Alexia! I'm Sparky, a little sprite of surprises! I've prepared something special for you today," Sparky said, with a twinkle in its eyes.

With a wave of its magical wand, Sparky created a gate in a tree nearby. The gate looked as if it led to another world full of mystery. Alexia stood there, her mouth agape, and her heart filled with emotion.

"Go ahead, Alexia! See where this gate of surprises will take you," Sparky invited, encouraging her to explore.

Filled with courage and excitement, Alexia passed through the gate and found herself in a breathtaking world. Bright colors, tall trees, and magical creatures surrounded her. In the midst of this magical land, Alexia found a mysterious box.

Sparky whispered that something special was inside the box, but to discover what it was, she needed to open it with a heart full of joy and curiosity. Alexia opened the box, and a radiant light flooded the entire world around her.

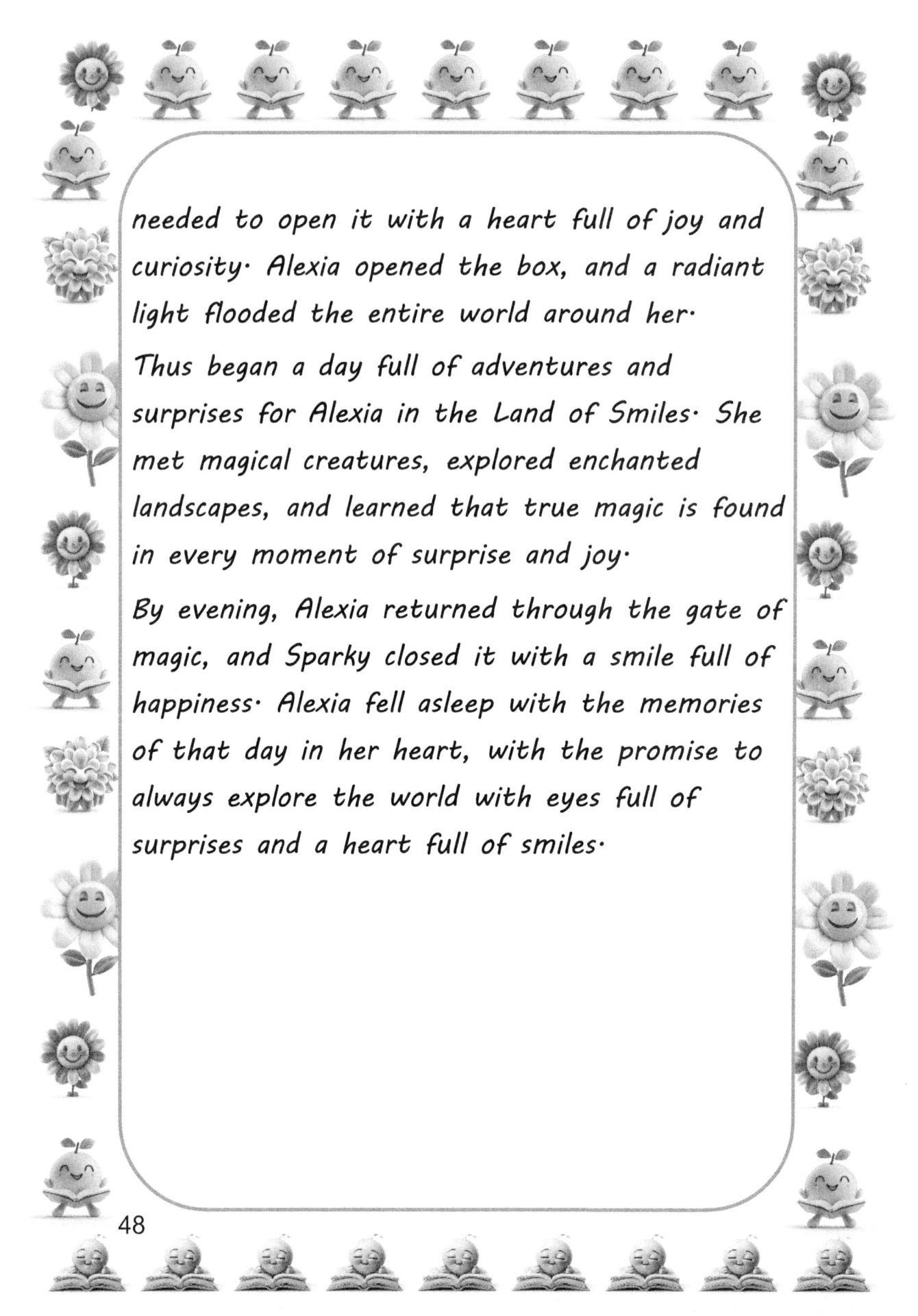

Thus began a day full of adventures and surprises for Alexia in the Land of Smiles. She met magical creatures, explored enchanted landscapes, and learned that true magic is found in every moment of surprise and joy.

By evening, Alexia returned through the gate of magic, and Sparky closed it with a smile full of happiness. Alexia fell asleep with the memories of that day in her heart, with the promise to always explore the world with eyes full of surprises and a heart full of smiles.

The emotion of contempt

It is a powerful feeling that many of us experience in certain situations. The emotion of contempt is a combination of rejection, disgust, and superiority towards something or someone. Let's start with how we feel when we experience contempt. It's like feeling that what you see or what happens to you is inferior or unacceptable. It can be like when someone does something you consider unfair or when you see something that deeply bothers you.

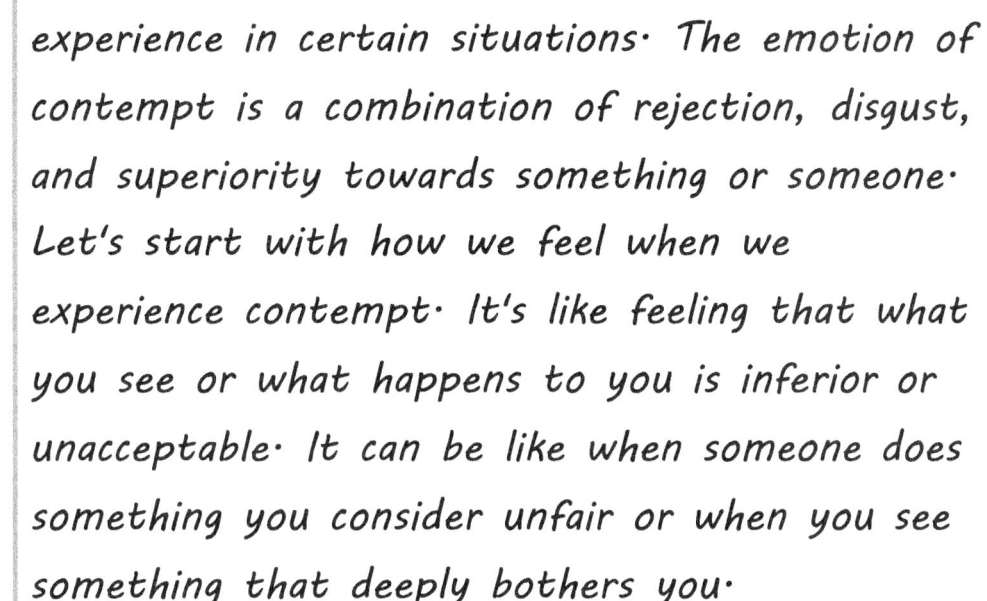

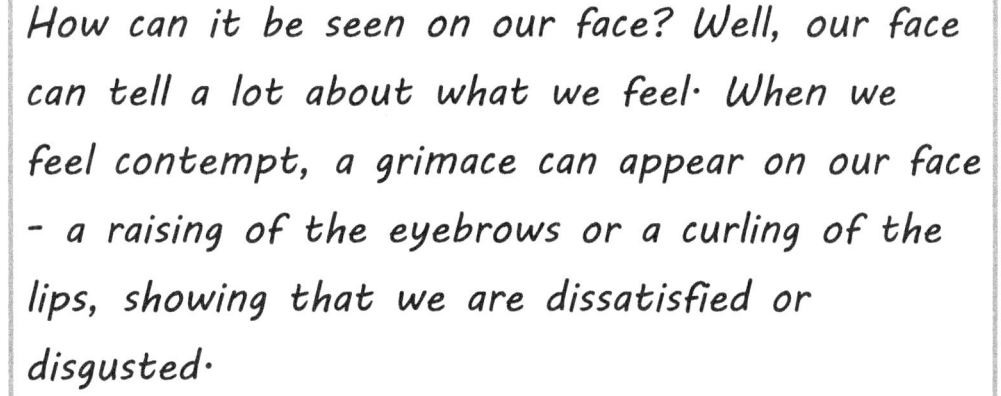

How can it be seen on our face? Well, our face can tell a lot about what we feel. When we feel contempt, a grimace can appear on our face - a raising of the eyebrows or a curling of the lips, showing that we are dissatisfied or disgusted.

Also, our body language can reveal much about what we feel. We can cross our arms or move away from the source of contempt. Sometimes, we can even shrug our shoulders in a sign of indifference or turn our backs.

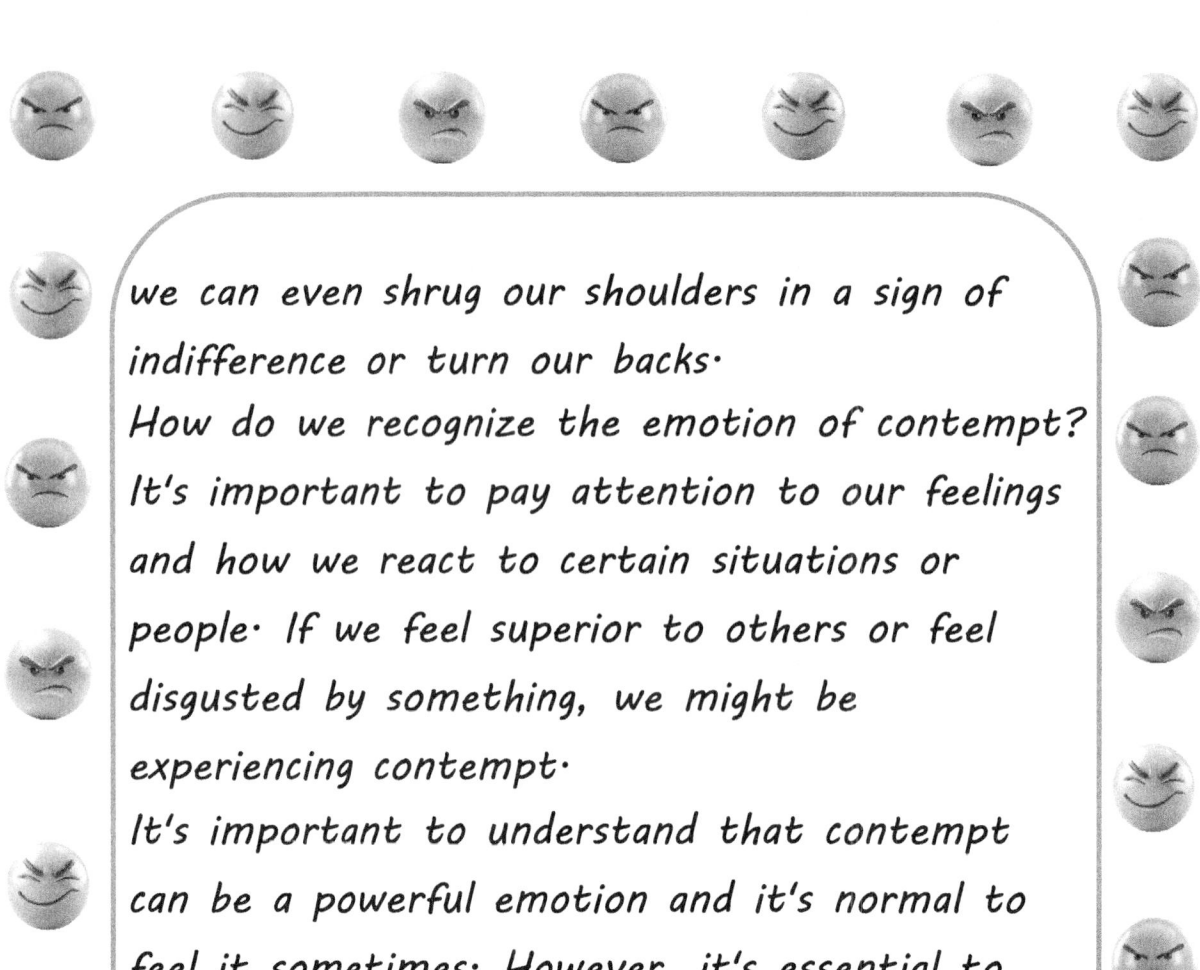

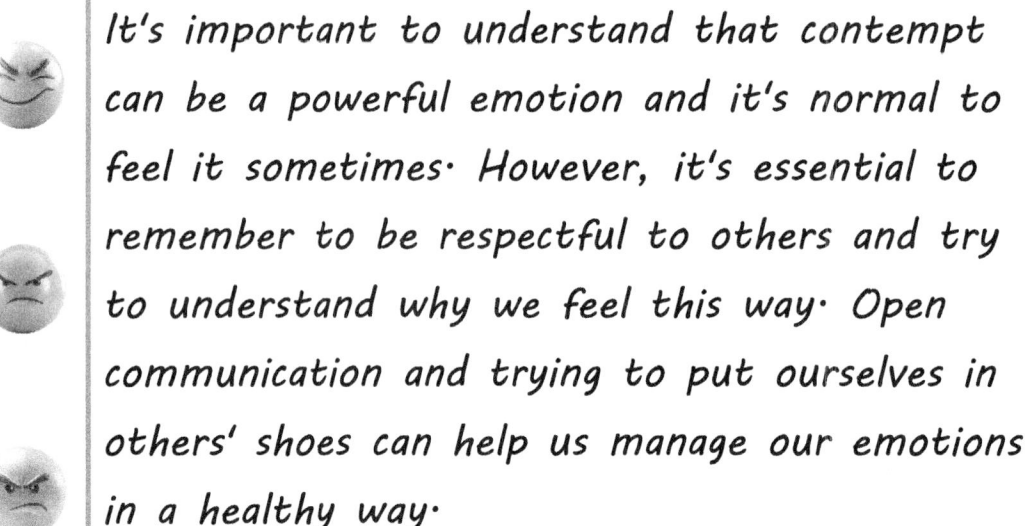

How do we recognize the emotion of contempt? It's important to pay attention to our feelings and how we react to certain situations or people. If we feel superior to others or feel disgusted by something, we might be experiencing contempt.

It's important to understand that contempt can be a powerful emotion and it's normal to feel it sometimes. However, it's essential to remember to be respectful to others and try to understand why we feel this way. Open communication and trying to put ourselves in others' shoes can help us manage our emotions in a healthy way.

I hope this information helps you better understand the emotion of contempt and how to recognize it when it arises. It's important to listen to and understand our feelings in order to manage our emotions in a positive and healthy way.

Managing Contempt Emotion

Acknowledge Your Feelings:
Learn to identify and name your emotions. When you feel contempt, say to yourself, "I feel contempt" and try to understand why you feel that way.

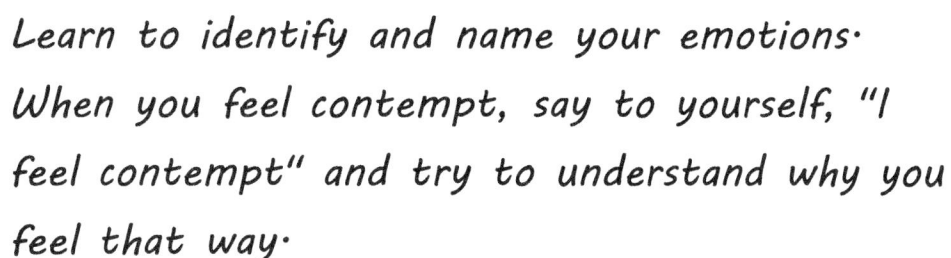

Talk About Your Feelings:
Don't be afraid to talk about how you feel with your parents or a trusted friend. Open communication can help release emotions.

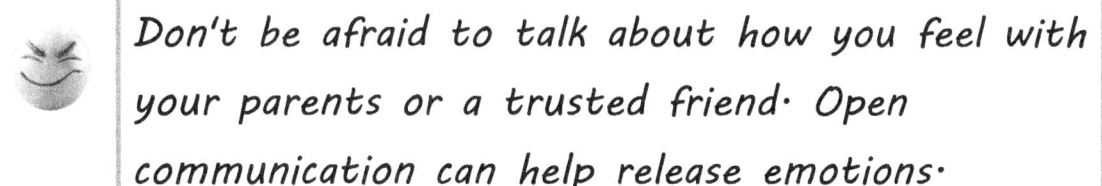

Deep Breaths:
Learn simple deep breathing techniques. You can try inhaling deeply through your nose and exhaling slowly through your mouth. This can help you calm down.

Draw or Write:
If you can't speak about your feelings, try drawing or writing about them. Doing this can help you release emotions and see the situation from a new perspective.

Focus on Positive Things:
Concentrate on the positive aspects of your day. Find things to be grateful for and enjoy them.

Engage in Pleasant Activities:
Find activities that make you happy and engage in them when you feel upset or disappointed. It could be reading a favorite book, drawing, or playing fun games.

Share with Others:
If you feel comfortable, share your feelings with your friends. Having someone listen to you can make a difference.

Learn About Empathy:
Understand that each person has their own feelings, and try to see situations from others' perspectives. Being empathetic can help avoid conflicts.

Set Realistic Goals:
Set realistic goals for yourself. Don't expect too much from yourself and have confidence that you can handle challenges.

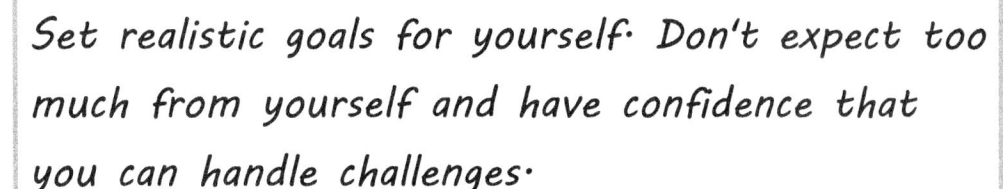

Be Friendly:
Try to be kind and help other kids. A smile or a kind gesture can change the entire atmosphere.

Seek Help When Needed:
If you feel that you can't manage your emotions alone, don't hesitate to ask for help from your parents, teacher, or a trusted adult.

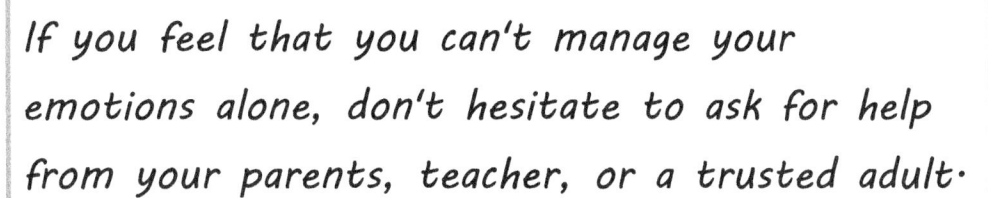

Remember that it's perfectly okay to feel various emotions, and learning how to manage them is part of our growth towards being a happier person.

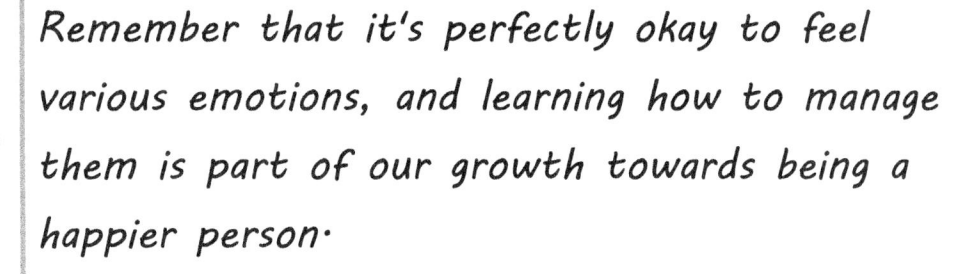

The Story of the Disgusting Flower

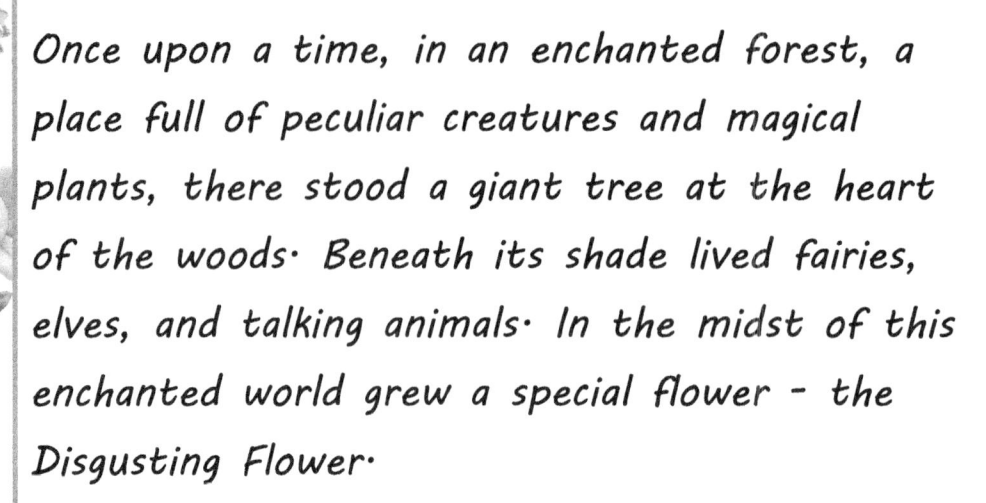

Once upon a time, in an enchanted forest, a place full of peculiar creatures and magical plants, there stood a giant tree at the heart of the woods. Beneath its shade lived fairies, elves, and talking animals. In the midst of this enchanted world grew a special flower - the Disgusting Flower.

The Disgusting Flower was known for its unpleasant smell and bizarre appearance. It had green and brown petals, and its fragrance could make anyone cover their nose. Despite its unusual look and scent, the Disgusting Flower was a loner and lived far away from other flowers.

One day, a group of curious little ones, comprised of fairies and elves, decided to explore the enchanted forest. During their adventure, they heard whispers about the Disgusting Flower and decided to seek it out to see what made it so unique.

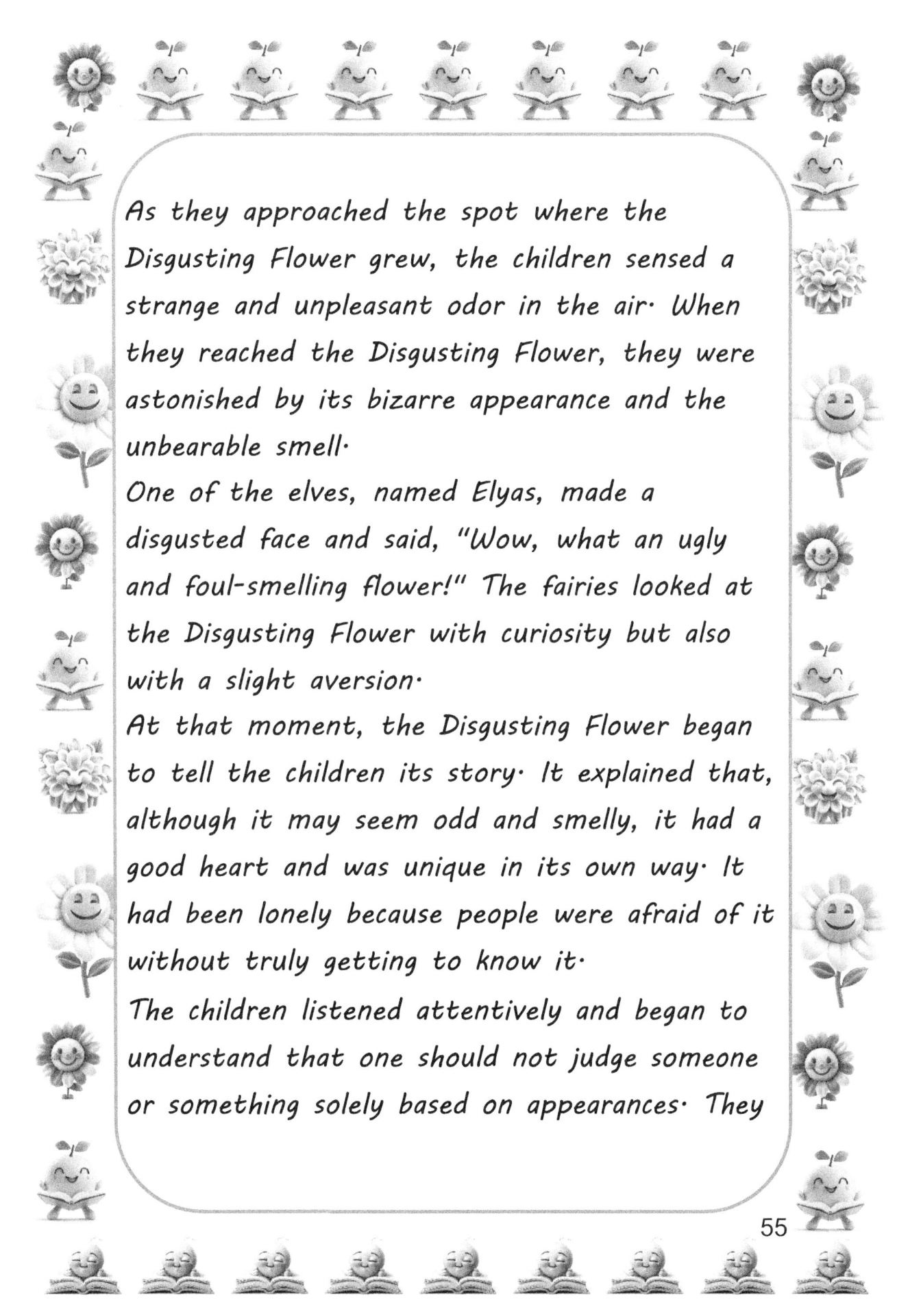

As they approached the spot where the Disgusting Flower grew, the children sensed a strange and unpleasant odor in the air. When they reached the Disgusting Flower, they were astonished by its bizarre appearance and the unbearable smell.

One of the elves, named Elyas, made a disgusted face and said, "Wow, what an ugly and foul-smelling flower!" The fairies looked at the Disgusting Flower with curiosity but also with a slight aversion.

At that moment, the Disgusting Flower began to tell the children its story. It explained that, although it may seem odd and smelly, it had a good heart and was unique in its own way. It had been lonely because people were afraid of it without truly getting to know it.

The children listened attentively and began to understand that one should not judge someone or something solely based on appearances. They decided to give the Disgusting Flower a chance to become their friend and learned to look beyond first impressions.

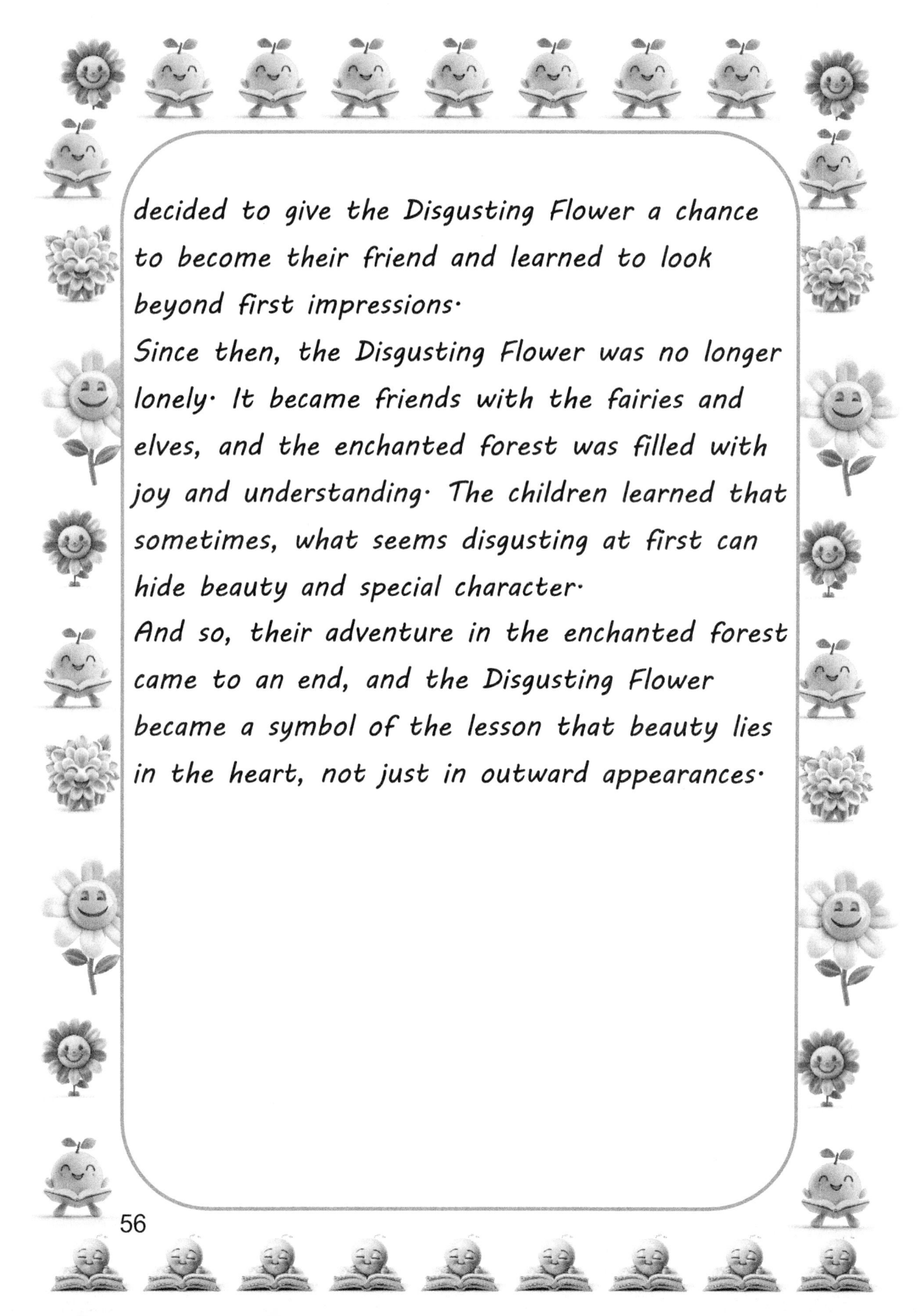

Since then, the Disgusting Flower was no longer lonely. It became friends with the fairies and elves, and the enchanted forest was filled with joy and understanding. The children learned that sometimes, what seems disgusting at first can hide beauty and special character.

And so, their adventure in the enchanted forest came to an end, and the Disgusting Flower became a symbol of the lesson that beauty lies in the heart, not just in outward appearances.

Dear Reader,

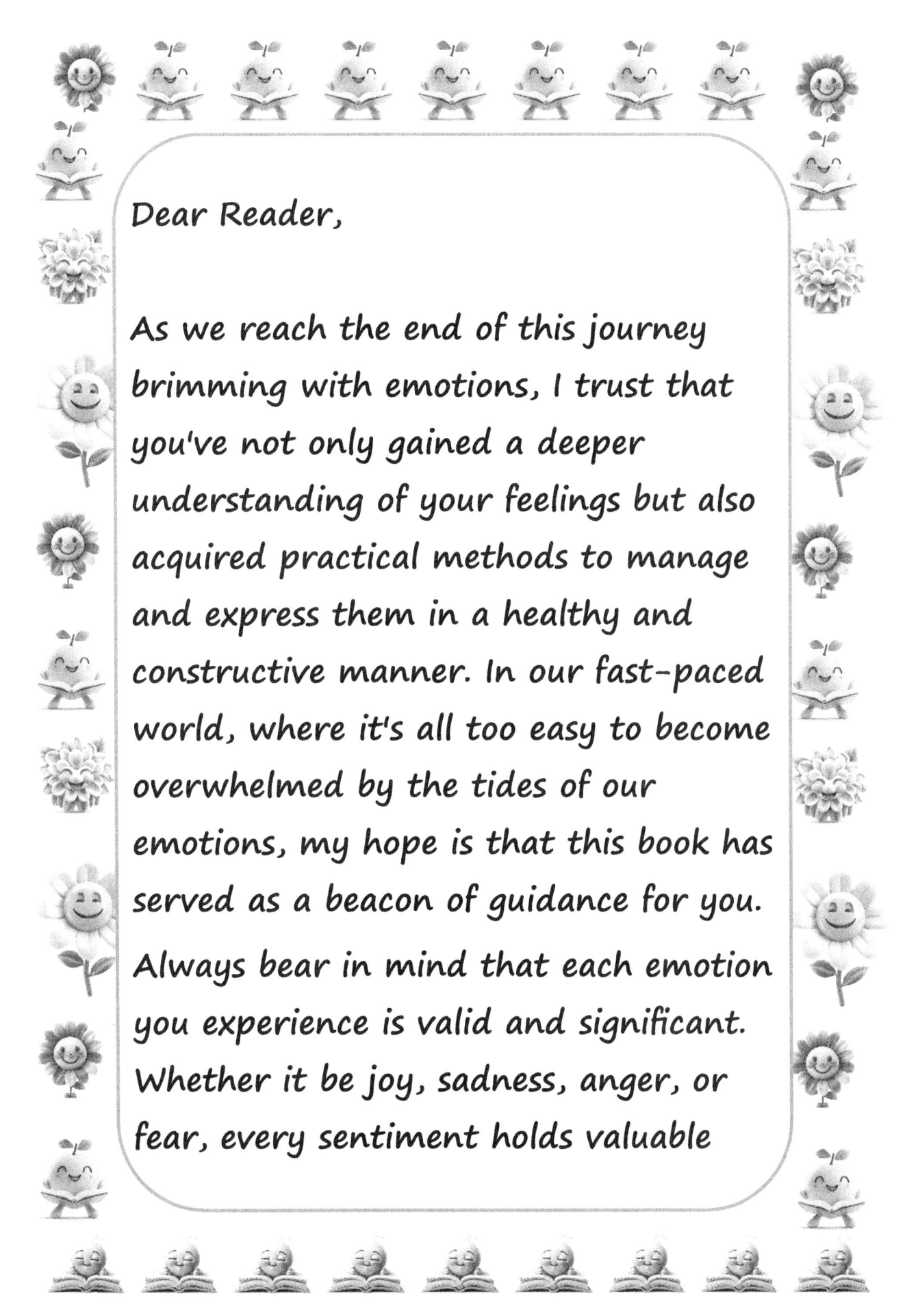

As we reach the end of this journey brimming with emotions, I trust that you've not only gained a deeper understanding of your feelings but also acquired practical methods to manage and express them in a healthy and constructive manner. In our fast-paced world, where it's all too easy to become overwhelmed by the tides of our emotions, my hope is that this book has served as a beacon of guidance for you.

Always bear in mind that each emotion you experience is valid and significant. Whether it be joy, sadness, anger, or fear, every sentiment holds valuable lessons and insights. Believe in yourselves and summon the courage to express your true selves authentically to the world.

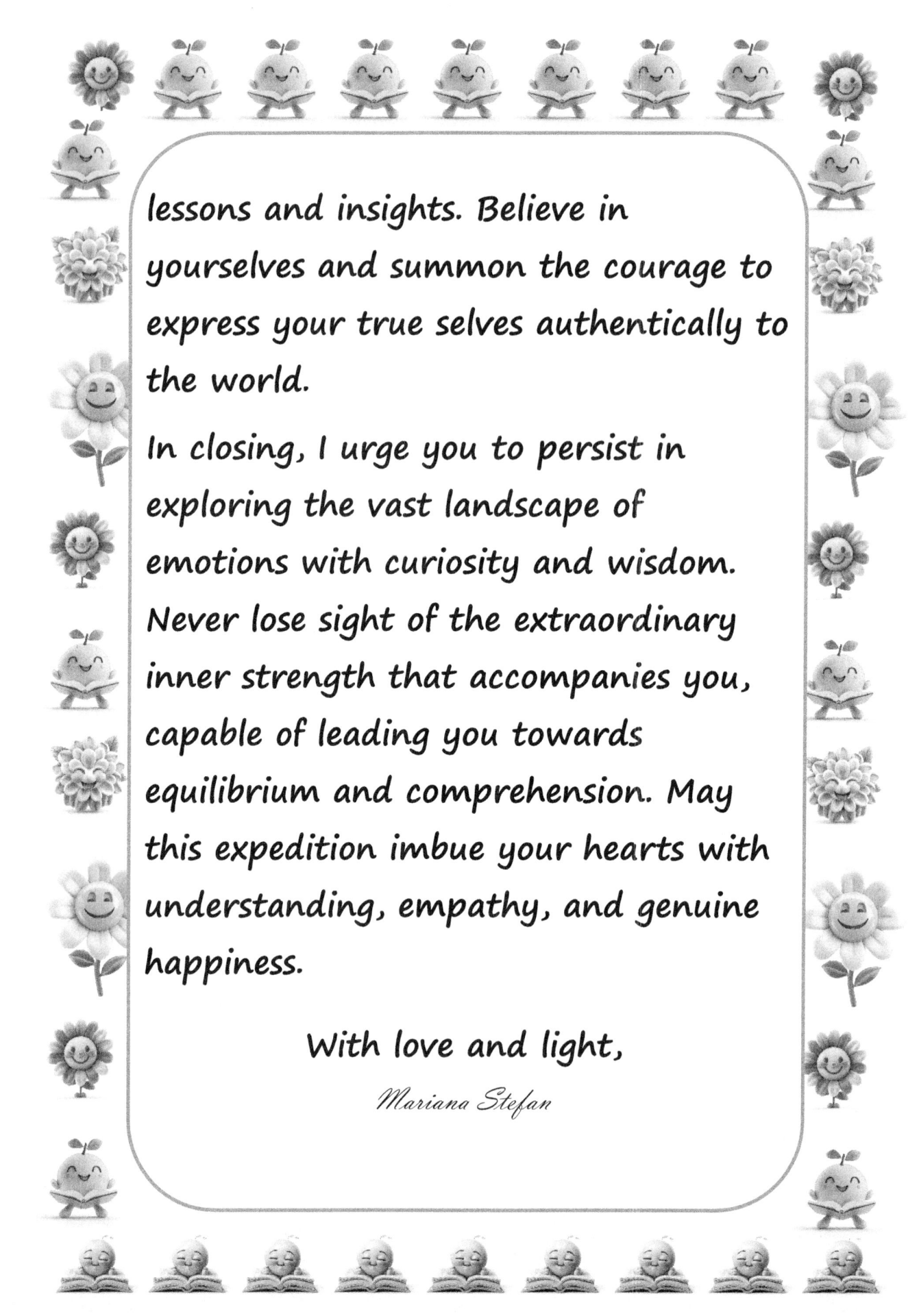

In closing, I urge you to persist in exploring the vast landscape of emotions with curiosity and wisdom. Never lose sight of the extraordinary inner strength that accompanies you, capable of leading you towards equilibrium and comprehension. May this expedition imbue your hearts with understanding, empathy, and genuine happiness.

With love and light,

Mariana Stefan

Printed in Great Britain
by Amazon